Japanese
Dress in Detail

Japanese Dress in Detail

Josephine Rout

with Anna Jackson

Frontispiece:
Fashionable Brocade Patterns
of the Imperial Palace
Utagawa Kunisada (1786–1864)
Colour print from woodblocks
1847–52
CIRC.636-1962

First published in the United Kingdom in 2020 by
Thames & Hudson Ltd, 181A High Holborn, London, WC1V 7QX
in association with the Victoria and Albert Museum, London

First published in the United States of America in 2020 by
Thames & Hudson Inc., 500 Fifth Avenue, New York,
New York 10110

Reprinted 2024

Japanese Dress in Detail © 2020 Victoria and Albert
Museum, London/Thames & Hudson Ltd, London

Text, V&A photographs and original line illustrations
© 2020 Victoria and Albert Museum, London
Design and layout © 2020 Thames & Hudson Ltd, London

British Library Cataloguing-in-Publication Data
A catalogue record for this book is available from
the British Library

Library of Congress Control Number 2019947906

ISBN 978-0-500-48057-1

Printed in China by RR Donnelley

Be the first to know about our new releases,
exclusive content and author events by visiting
thamesandhudson.com
thamesandhudsonusa.com
thamesandhudson.com.au

V&A Publishing
Supporting the world's leading
museum of art and design,
the Victoria and Albert
Museum, London

Contents

伊勢崎銘仙
千代田御召

INTRODUCTION

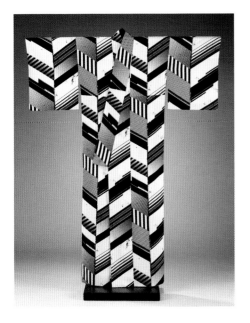

Throughout the history of Japanese dress, crucial information about the wearer can be found in the details. Age, status and taste are carefully communicated through the silent language of clothing in both overt and subtle ways. Detail is particularly important when examining the kimono, the straight-seamed, T-shaped garment that epitomizes Japanese sartorial identity and translates as 'a thing worn'. They are made from a single bolt of cloth and when constructed are wrapped around the body, left side over right, and secured with a sash called an *obi*. Although the basic shape has not changed, the combination of materials, decorative techniques, patterns and way of wearing the garment varies drastically.

Most forms of clothing recognizable as Japanese were based on imported Chinese styles and adapted during the Heian period (784–1185). However, it was during the Edo period (1615–1868), that Japanese dress, in particular the kimono, flourished due to the development of a highly sophisticated fashion system. As the most important aspect of Japanese dress is the surface decoration, it is the scale and placement of pattern that changes, as do the ways in which they are applied. The beauty of many kimono is the combination of multiple decorative techniques, including weaving, dyeing, painting and embroidery. In many cases, it is the technique that allows us to date a kimono. Lavishly embroidered satin kimono (pp. 150 and 151), for example, are characteristic of the mid-19th century, while machine-spun stencil-dyed kimono, known as *meisen* (p. 93), defined early 20th-century style. Today, inkjet printing is one of the latest developments in kimono design (below, left).

The generic term kimono was once not so widely used. It was adopted relatively recently during the Meiji period (1868–1912) in tandem with the introduction of western clothing, referred to as *yōfuku*, thereby creating the category of Japanese dress (*wafuku*). Until then, kimono were more than simply 'a thing worn', but everyday dress for all genders and classes, further defined by specific details. Many of the different dress terms pertain to the sleeve, such as *kosode* (small sleeve), *ōsode* (large sleeve) and *furisode* (fluttering sleeve). Kimono were worn with other types of garments, such as *hakama* (pleated trousers or skirts) and *haori* (kimono-style jackets), together with various accessories including combs, fans and tobacco pouches. Rather than being chronological, this book has been arranged around different elements of clothing, from hair ornaments to undergarments and footwear, each section providing a different angle from which to examine the intricacies of Japanese dress.

The Victoria and Albert Museum has been collecting examples of Japanese clothing since 1871 and now has one of the most important holdings outside Japan. This introduction provides an overview of the main periods of Japanese fashion history represented in the collection. This is by no means diverse nor exhaustive; women's dress predominates as do the clothes of the upper middle classes, particularly those made for special occasions such as weddings. However, an attempt has been made to include a broad range of clothing, including clothing for men and children, regional styles and garments used for court, performance and ceremonial occasions. In recent years, the Victoria and Albert Museum has been actively acquiring examples of contemporary Japanese dress at all levels, from kimono made by Living National Treasures to young designers working with digital technology.

Edo: The First Fashion City

When Tokugawa Ieyasu (1542–1616), the warrior governor of Japan (*shōgun*), moved the military capital to Edo (now Tokyo), a small swamp town in Eastern Japan, he unwittingly founded one of the first fashion cities. While Kyoto remained the imperial capital, Edo, after which this significant period of Japanese history is named (1615–1867), quickly grew into the world's largest metropolis. It was an era defined by peace, political stability and the strict feudal hierarchy imposed and reinforced by the samurai, the Japanese military class. Based on Confucian principles, it placed the samurai firmly at the top, followed by farmers, then artisans, producers of food and products respectively, with merchants, those who simply profited from the work of others, at the bottom. However, it was the merchants who prospered and as a result sought to flaunt their wealth through clothing. People based in urban areas, such as artisans and merchants, were referred to as city dwellers (*chōnin*), and in many ways it was they who led culture. The fashion leaders of the day were not the ruling classes, but those within the fluid and dynamic 'floating world' (*ukiyo*) of urban Edo, such as kabuki actors and courtesans. Yet despite the Tokugawa Shogunate's attempts to thwart public desire for changing styles and luxurious materials, fashion became a driving economic and social force.

After centuries of catering to the imperial court and acting as the centre of textile production, Kyoto was geographically distanced from the Edo fashion system and became reliant upon national networks of design dissemination. Kimono pattern books, known as *hinagata bon* and first dated to 1666 (below), became not only an essential tool in design transmission between the makers in Kyoto and clients in Edo, but evidence that a fashion system was in formation.

OPPOSITE

Surugao-chō from the series *One Hundred Famous Views of Edo* by Utagawa Hiroshige (1797–1858). Colour print from woodblocks, Edo (Tokyo), 1856. E.4271-1886

BELOW

Kimono patterns by Hishikawa Moronobu (c. 1618–94). Book printed from woodblocks, Edo (Tokyo), 1675–85. Given by the Misses Alexander E.6844-1916.

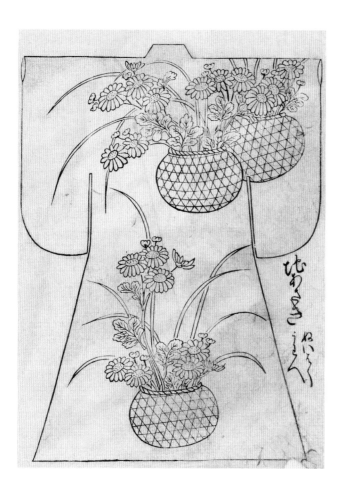

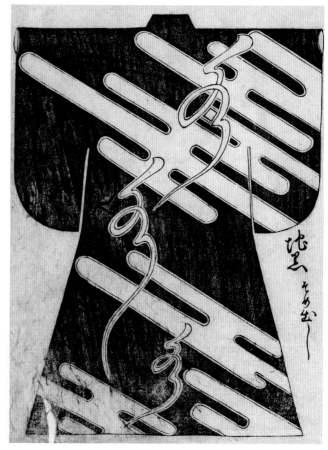

Merchants responded to this desire for fashionable dress with great zeal. Kimono shops, such as the Echigoya, employed the marketing strategies of branding and product placement in woodblock prints and books, the mass media of the time. Founded by Mitsui Takatoshi (1622–94) in 1673, the Echigoya logo could be found in various prints, such is on the shopfront curtains (*noren*) in this view of Mount Fuji by Hiroshige (previous page), or on the wrappers of this merchant's textile samples (right). Takatoshi also recognized the power of celebrity and ensured his products were associated with the famous faces of the floating world.

At the start of the Edo period, imported Chinese silks epitomized luxury and were consumed in large quantities by high-ranking samurai. Such textiles greatly influenced the costumes of the *Nō* theatre, an esoteric form of musical drama, as they were gifted to actors by samurai patrons (pp. 30 and 90). While Chinese figured silks and crêpes were ideal for kimono, such trade was depleting Japan's reserves of precious metals. The Tokugawa government attempted to decrease this desire for foreign cloth and replace it with an improved domestic sericulture (silk cultivation). Raw silk production occurred in various parts of Japan but it was in Kyoto, particularly the Nishijin district, where silk was made into luxurious textiles for clothing. Kyoto had the most skilled artisans as well as the ideal natural resources for creating dyes. It was also in Kyoto that *yūzen*, a sophisticated freehand paste resist-dyeing technique, developed, allowing artisans to draw patterns directly onto the cloth. *Yūzen* was named after the artist Miyazaki Yūzen (1654?–1736), a fan painter whose kimono designs were published in 1688 to great appeal. Although not necessarily a dyer, the technique named after Yūzen transformed kimono design.

Silk was ostensibly out of reach for those below samurai status. The vast majority of the population were prohibited, both legally and economically, from wearing silk, and were thus limited to wearing home-spun bast fibres, such as hemp, flax and wisteria. It was the successful cultivation of cotton from the late 16th century that drastically transformed dress for the lower echelons of society. In contrast to coarse and labour-intensive bast fibres, cotton was softer, warmer and easier to decorate. It was also relatively straightforward to manufacture and its popularity throughout the country resulted in a sophisticated trade network. Domestic trade was essential to the economy as the Tokugawa government had

ABOVE
An Echigo-ya Merchant Visiting Two Women, from the series *The Cultivation of Silk Worm* by Katsukawa Shunshō (1726–92). Colour print from woodblocks, Edo (Tokyo), 1786. E.1360-1922

BELOW LEFT
Sarasa Handbook, enlarged edition [Zohō Sarasa Benran] by Hōrai Sanjin Kikyō and Kusumi Magozaemon (active 1750–1800). Book printed from woodblocks, Edo (Tokyo), 1781. Given by the Misses Alexander E.6924-1916.

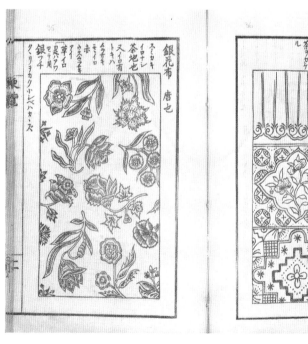
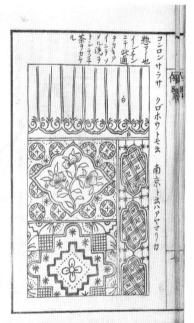

ABOVE
Fireworks at Ryōgoku Bridge by Utagawa Toyokuni
(1769–1825). Colour print from woodblocks, Edo (Tokyo),
1820–5. E.4900-1886

instituted a strict closed country policy, known as *sakoku*. However, there were some exceptions to this ruling as the Dutch were allowed to trade in Deijima, an island near the port town of Nagasaki. The South and South-East Asian printed cotton textiles brought by the Dutch were highly sought after as rare and exotic. Known as *sarasa*, Japanese artisans started producing their own versions using stencils (*wa-sarasa*) to supply demand (p. 10, below).

The growth of the merchant class during the Edo period, coupled with the declining fortunes of low-ranking samurai, resulted in a complex battle between official attempts to maintain class distinctions and the economic imperative of capitalism. Ostentatious display desired by wealthy merchants and the denizens of the entertainment districts was thwarted by sumptuary laws, most of which pertained to colour, material and technique. Although many flouted such rules, urban commoners created an aesthetic around the muted colour palette to which they were limited. Dark brown, grey and indigo cottons came to define a new fashion known as *iki*. Like many trends today, *iki* was not simply about what one wore, but how it was worn and by whom. Such emphasis on style reveals that getting dressed during the Edo period, when even the smallest details would be noticed, was by no means simple.

Fashioning 'Modern' Japan

After Japan was officially 'reopened' to the world in 1853, a concerted effort was made to 'catch up' with the West. One of the main aims of the new Emperor Meiji (1852–1912), who was restored to the throne in 1868, was to radically transform the country by way of industrial development, military power and social progress. Japan was self-conscious regarding its own image and saw western clothing as a way to prove that the nation was equal to European and American powers. The promotion of western dress was neither straightforward nor comprehensive, resulting in a hybrid style that incorporated Japanese and western elements (right). This reflected the public discourse, dominated by phrases such as *wakon-yōsai* ('Japanese spirit, western techniques'), a theory that was applied to dress in equal measure as it was to the military or industry.

The first form of western clothing to be formally adopted in Japan was uniforms for the military and government officials. This included the Meiji emperor, who donned such dress to project modernity and encourage his compatriots to do the same. While western dress had been successfully adopted for men, the promotion of such styles was not a simple matter for women and went through various permutations. In 1887 the empress issued an edict urging her countrywomen to adopt western clothing, yet to have it made in local materials by local dressmakers. However, trading kimono for western dress was at odds with Japanese notions of morality and health. The elaborate S-curve shape fashionable at the time not only exaggerated the female form, but also required a tightened corset to create a wasp waist. So bewildered were the Japanese by this, it made them hesitant to clothe young women in such garb. Conversely, kimono were becoming an essential item for the wardrobes of fashionable women in the West. While initially these were kimono that had been made for samurai women – a market no longer in existence after the abolishment of the feudal class system in 1871 – astute merchants were soon supplying kimono specially made for export, many of which had extra gored panels so that they could be worn over petticoats (opposite).

Domestically, the kimono was modernized using new materials and technology. The textiles sector was the first to industrialize; this was a timely move as Japan was able to swiftly supply Europe with raw silk following the pébrine epidemic that wiped out silkworms throughout the continent. Silk would grow to be Japan's leading export. Artisans from Kyoto travelled to Europe to study the jacquard loom while the recently invented chemical dyes, accidentally discovered by William Henry Perkins (1838–1907) in 1856, were swiftly adopted and then developed in Japan from the 1860s with the assistance of European experts. A Department of Chemistry (*Seimi Kyoku*) was established in Kyoto in

ABOVE
View of Nihon-bashi in Tokyo by Utagawa Kuniteru
(1830–74). Colour print from woodblocks, Tokyo, 1870.
E.99-1969

RIGHT
Kimono for export, retailed in Europe or America. Silk
satin (*shusu*); embroidery in silk threads, probably Kyoto,
1905–15. FE.46-2018

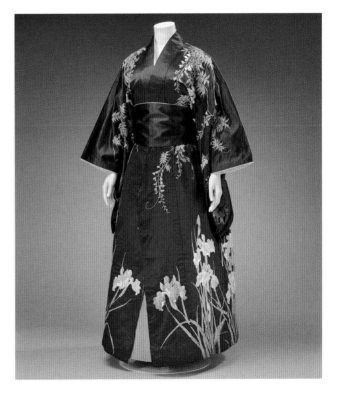

OPPOSITE
Design for kimono. Plain-weave silk; freehand paste resist-dyeing; hand-painting in ink and colours; embroidery in silk and gold-wrapped silk threads, probably Kyoto, c. 1900. E.713-1901

BELOW
Summer kimono for a woman. Gauze-weave silk (ro); stencil-dyeing. Probably Isesaki, 1910–30. Given by Moe Co. Ltd. FE.146-2002.

1870 to undertake research into dyes and five years later the *Somedono* (Dyeing Palace) was created to teach artisans the necessary skills. The vast array of colours now available did not have an overt impact on fashion, with many preferring the subdued colours of the late Edo period. However, chemical dyes, which were used for prints as well as textiles, were to be found in subtle details, such as supplementary embroidery or silk linings (opposite).

This would change as Japan entered the 20th century with great cultural confidence and sartorial bravado, having defeated Russia in the Russo-Japanese War in 1905 and profiting from the global demand for resources during the First World War. This mood of optimism and affluence coincided with the new imperial reign, thus becoming the Taishō period (1912–26) and was reflected through the

eclectic array of fashion available and new types of people wearing them.
Many leading kimono merchants established department stores, such as the
Echigoya, which became Mitsukoshi in 1904. These new shops changed the
way that people bought clothes by offering ready-to-wear garments and were
fundamental in the promotion of global fashions such as art nouveau and art
deco. Japan not only looked beyond its borders, but also to the nation's past
for inspiration, resulting in a revival for the flamboyant fashions of the Genroku
era (1688–1704), made even more vibrant with the aid of chemical dyes.

ABOVE
Kimono for an infant boy. Plain-weave silk; hand-painting
in ink and colours (*kaki-e*); stencil-dyeing; embroidery
in silk and metallic threads, 1930–45. FE. 45-2014

The early decades of the 20th century were also defined by the development of a new type of kimono known as *meisen*. Inexpensive and durable, *meisen* are made from the thick silk thread of deformed cocoons and machine spun. The patterning of *meisen* was also the result of modern techniques; chemical dyes mixed with rice paste were applied directly to warp-and-weft threads before weaving, thus creating bold effects. The sheer variety of designs and colour combinations found on *meisen* kimono reveal how creative and rapid production was, reflecting the latest fashions and current events. Advertisements featuring popular actresses wearing *meisen* (p. 6) were designed to appeal to young, urban women including *moga*, the modern girls who cut their hair short and frequented jazz clubs.

The Great Kantō earthquake of 1923 destroyed most of Tokyo and foreshadowed the difficulties that were to follow. As Japan's military ambitions in Asia increased the economy declined, resulting in fertile ground for fascist ideology. While the nation prepared for war, militant nationalism was found in all aspects of life, including dress. Novelty prints incorporated propaganda motifs such as warplanes and battleships (opposite), while women were discouraged from wearing silk kimono and instead adopted the garb of rural workers such as *monpe* trousers.

Japanese Dress in a Globalized World

Following the tumultuous years of the Pacific War (1941–5), the wearing of kimono drastically declined, going from daily wear to a form of ceremonial costume. While this sartorial shift affected all aspects of Japanese dress, the most significant change was cognitive. Garments such as kimono became associated with tradition while western clothing signified contemporary Japan. Emphasis was placed on highly formal kimono for special occasions, such as the coming-of-age day and weddings. In addition, the expense of kimono meant that they came to be appreciated as objects to be admired, particularly as examples of Japanese craftsmanship, rather than something to be worn.

The decline in daily kimono wear meant that most people lost the ability to dress themselves in kimono. Like many forms of culture threatened with extinction, Japanese dress was carefully codified, to the point that the custom of wearing kimono is more complicated than it was when it had been an item of everyday dress. This was mostly the work of kimono schools, which taught how to wear kimono (*kitsuke*), and were established in the 1960s. Aimed at women, their prescriptive methods, which often involved numerous underpinnings (*komono*) in order to achieve a perfectly cylindrical form, were for many intimidating and off-putting. That they taught etiquette as well as *obi*-tying meant that the kimono came to epitomize conservative Japanese femininity rather than items of forms of fashionable dress. Instead, it became associated with other forms of traditional art, such as the tea ceremony and flower arranging.

In parallel to this shift, the Japanese Government was wary of losing such important aspects of its culture and in the 1950s instituted a system to preserve intangible cultural assets. Commonly referred to as 'Living National Treasures' (Ningen Kokuhō), the individuals conferred with this title conserve and develop techniques that would otherwise be at risk of being lost. The kimono continues to be the ideal site for dyers and weavers to express their skill and create garments of exceptional beauty. Although most of these kimono are made for exhibition and may never actually be worn, for people such as Moriguchi Kunihiko (b. 1941), Living National Treasure for *yūzen* dyeing, it is imperative that the kimono remains an item of dress as well as a work of art (overleaf).

Despite notions that kimono are costly, conventional and at odds with contemporary life, the 21st century ushered in a kimono revival led by Japanese youth. Unlike the generation above them, today's kimono wearers approach the garment and other items of Japanese dress as items of fashion with which to have fun. This trend started with vintage kimono from the Taishō and early

BELOW

The Book of Kimono: The Complete Guide to Style and Wear by Norio Yamanaka, Kodansha International, Tokyo, 1982. National Art Library at the V&A: 38041801449380

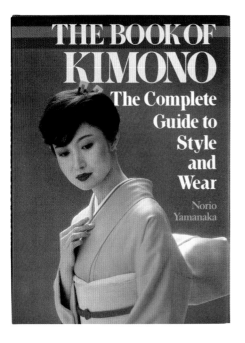

OPPOSITE

Kimono for a woman (*hōmongi*) entitled *Grey of Dawn* by Moriguchi Kunihiko (b .1941). Silk crêpe, freehand paste resist-dyeing (*yūzen*), Kyoto, 1987. FE.421-1992

RIGHT

Summer kimono (*yukata*) ensemble for a woman by Hiroko Takahashi (b. 1977). Kimono: inkjet; cotton linen slab, made in Tōkamachi, Niigata prefecture, 2010. *Obi: hakata* brocade, silk made in Fukuoka, 2009. Shoes (*geta*): paulownia; lacquer; deerskin made in Aizu, Fukushima prefecture, 2009. Courtesy of Hiroko Takahashi.

Shōwa periods (1926–89) that are affordable and widely available. Inspired by the lively fashions and relaxed way of dressing of these earlier times, young Japanese people have been learning about how to wear kimono but also have created confidence amongst kimono wearers to break the rules. This has been facilitated by the internet, where an online community has developed into a global network of kimono enthusiasts keen to share knowledge and exchange ideas. A new wave of designers has come out of this revival and are approaching kimono design in fresh and subversive ways, using digital printing or contemporary motifs to make kimono relevant and accessible for today and the future.

Indeed, Japan's rich fashion culture is deeply indebted to its dynamic sartorial history and is what provides such great potential for *wafuku* to evolve. From the Edo period to the present, this book seeks to explore the various details that make Japanese dress so fascinating and compelling.

1. Necklines and Shoulders

Jacket for a man (*jimbaori*)
Wool; lined with silk; silk braid;
stencilled deerskin
1800–50

T.136-1964

This jacket is a *jimbaori* and was worn by a high-ranking samurai over his armour. *Jimbaori* developed in the 16th century but, by the time this example was made, Japan was at peace and such garments no longer needed to withstand the rigours of the battlefield, being worn instead purely for ceremony. This *jimbaori* is made from woollen cloth imported from Europe that has been treated and shrunk giving it a felt-like look and texture. On the back in black-wool appliqué is the samurai's family crest. The extravagant epaulettes, one of which is shown in this detail, are constructed of layers of stiff paper covered with stencilled deerskin, gold wrapped cord, black and purple wool and blue braid. Silk braiding, known as *kumihimo*, has been used as both a form of decoration across the shoulders and to fasten the buttons holding the front lapels.

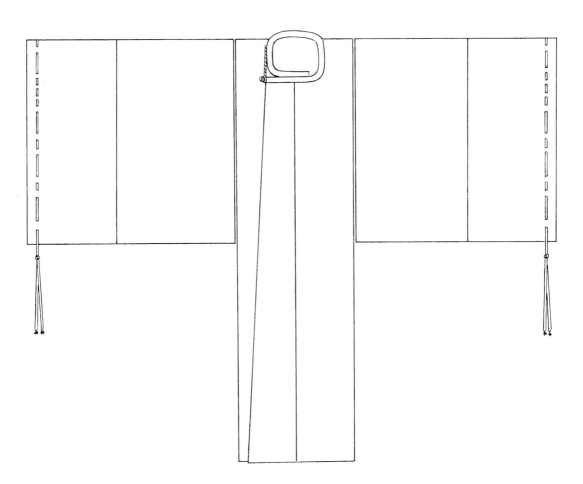

This double-breasted robe with its high, round collar, would have been worn by a male member of the Japanese imperial court. Layers of thick paper under the silk have made the collar very stiff, and twisted paper has also been used for the toggle and loop fastening. The clothing styles of the court were established in the Heian period (794–1185) and changed little over the succeeding centuries. This robe dates from the late 19th century and is called a *kariginu* (hunting cloak), although it was no longer worn for this purpose. The body of the garment is very narrow and open at the sides, which would have revealed the garments worn underneath. The double-width sleeves are attached only at the upper back, originally to allow for maximum ease of movement when drawing a bow on horseback. Cords threaded along the cuffs allow the sleeves to be gathered up. The garment was worn with a sash, drawn up slightly to make the front section shorter than the back.

Robe for a man (*kariginu*)
Figured twill silk (*mon aya*)
Probably Kyoto, 1850–1900

FE.158-1983

Robe for a man (*attush*)
Elm-bark fibre (*ohyō*) with cotton
appliqué, and embroidered in cotton
Hokkaido, 1850–1900

Given by Bernard Leach, CBE
T.99-1963

The thorn-like motifs that decorate the back of this robe were placed
to protect the wearer against evil spirits and would have been worn
by a man conducting an Ainu religious ritual. As the indigenous people
of Hokkaidō, the northernmost island of Japan, the Ainu have a culture
distinct from that of the mainland. This was reflected in their clothing,
that was imbued with their animist beliefs and made from locally
sourced materials. This robe, known as an *attush*, is woven from fibres
taken from the inner bark of the elm tree.

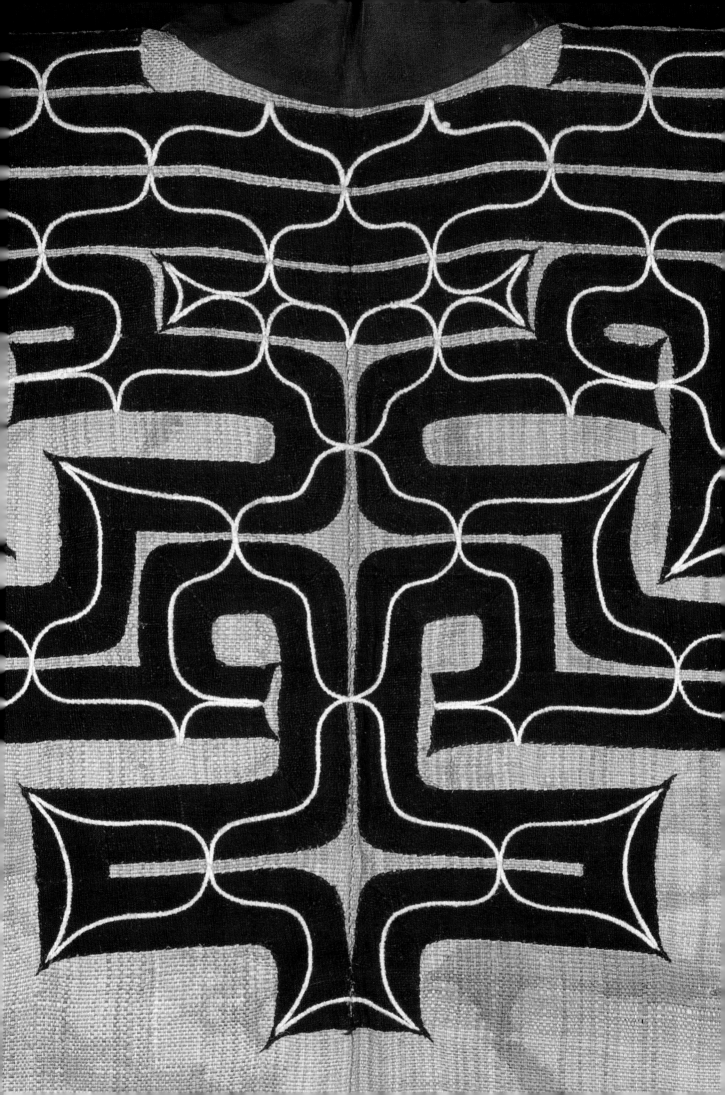

Children's garments often feature protective stitching, such as this kimono which has embroidered amulets (*kazari-nui*) at the collar where the ties are attached. Worked in orange silk thread, the stitching contrasts with the dark green ties that are made of cotton, stencil-dyed with chrysanthemums on a striated ground. The kimono itself is a highly sophisticated garment of freehand paste resist-dyed silk decorated in the *goshodoki* (palace-court) style. On the back, rippling water runs below a pine tree and through clusters of irises, a flower associated with *The Tales of Ise,* a famous 10th-century work of classical literature. *Goshodoki* patterns were reserved for members of the ruling samurai class for whom dress was highly regulated, even for children.

Kimono for a young girl
Plain-weave silk; freehand paste resist-dyeing
Probably Kyoto, 1800–50

FE.192-2018

Robe for *Nō* theatre (*kariginu*)
Gold figured silk (*kinran*)
Probably Kyoto, 1750–1850

FE.8-1984

Nō is an esoteric form of theatre patronized by the samurai. Far removed from daily life, *Nō* plays focused on historic tales of the court life suffused with the supernatural. As the genre codified over time, certain roles called for specific costumes. The aristocratic styles and sumptuous fabrics used for *Nō* costumes are thought to have originated from the custom of patrons gifting their clothes to the actors. Richly woven with green silk and supplementary wefts of gilt paper strips (*kinran*), this striking garment has a bold design of hexagonal tortoiseshell (*kikkō*), 16-petalled chrysanthemums (*kiku*) and flaming wheel roundels containing triple-comma motifs (*mitsu-tomoe*). The neckline is fastened with a toggle and the sleeves are attached with silk cord. Gold brocades such as this were used for characters of noble rank.

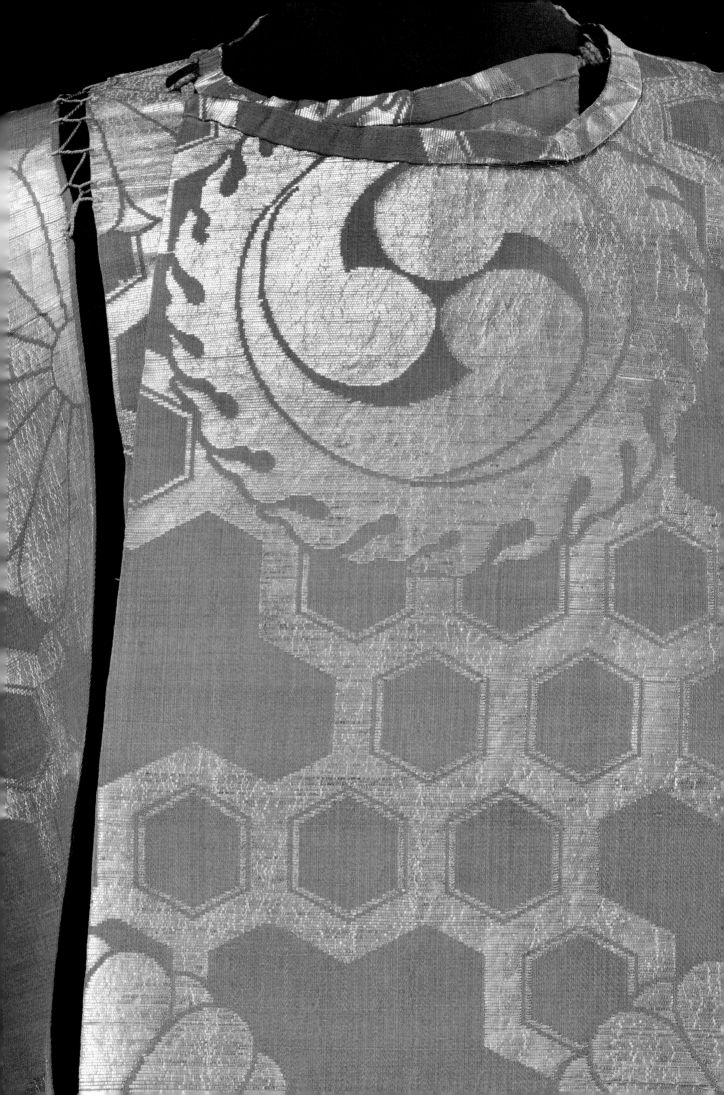

Pleated, starched and stiffened with paper, these exaggerated shoulders signify power. They form the top part of ceremonial dress for high-ranking samurai, an ensemble known as a *kamishimo*. The two-piece, which would be worn over a kimono, consists of an upper garment, called a *kataginu*, and pleated trousers (*hakama*). The two vertical panels at the front of the *kataginu* would have been tucked into the *hakama*, which have narrow ties and a waist board designed to give support to the back. The pleats of the *hakama*, five in front and two at the back, are believed to symbolize the virtues of a samurai: courage, benevolence, justice, courtesy, sincerity, loyalty and honour. Made of bast fibres such as hemp, rather than silk, the subtle stencil-dyed pattern of sharkskin (*same*) is a style known as *Edo komon*. The areas for the family crest (*mon*), were reserved with paste and then brushed with pigments. This samurai's crest is a chrysanthemum surrounded by two leaves and appears on the front and back of the *kataginu* and the back board of the *hakama*.

Two-piece garment (*kamishimo*) probably for a boy
Plain-weave bast fibre (*asa*); stencil paste resist-dyed (*kata-zome*) 1800–80

FE.46&A-1980

Kimono for a boy

Plain-weave silk; stencil-dyeing
(*kata-yūzen*); applied gold;
embroidery in metallic threads
c. 1970–90s

Donated by Teppei, Allison and Kye Otsuka
in memory of Shigeru and Hideko Sakamoto
FE.107-2018

Two family crests (*mon*) appear on the front of this kimono for a young boy, with three more on the back, making it a highly formal garment. The clover-shaped leaves surrounded by points within a circle is a crest known as the *maru no ken katabami*. Red-and-white silk embroidered amulets (*kazari-nui*) adorn the ties and provide protection to the young child. On the back of the garment a magnificent hawk rests on a rock, the feathers highlighted with supplementary embroidery, surrounded by pine and bamboo with waves crashing below. Birds of prey were historically associated with samurai but are now often used as motifs for boy's garments. Ceremonial children's wear is highly codified, with boys' kimono mostly made in dark colours and decorated with symbols that denote strength and courage. This garment was worn by Kye Otsuka as a baby for his first visit to a shrine, the *omiyamairi* ceremony, and then later at five years of age for the *shichi-go-san* ceremony, a day when parents take their children to a shrine to pray for their health and happiness.

This garment would have been worn by a samurai firefighter not for fighting a blaze but for ceremonial occasions. Known as a *kajibanten*, it consists of a jacket with chest protector (*muneate*) and sash. It is woven from *kuzu* fibre, extracted from the inner bark of the arrowroot. The bast fibre was not cultivated and preparing it for weaving was a labour-intensive process. The stiff texture and open weave made it ideal for formal summer clothing. Dark brown silk cord has been used to decorate and edge all three sections of the ensemble. The prominent family crest, an orange blossom within a circle (*tachibana*), adorns the bib and shoulders of the jacket.

Coat and chest-protector for a firefighter (*kajibanten*)
Plain-weave *kuzu* fibre with applied decoration
1750–1850

FE.27-1984

Kimono for a child
Plain-weave silk woven with selectively
pre-dyed yarns (*kasuri*)
1870–1910

FE.51-1982

This attractive striped kimono is made using a technique known as
kasuri. Similar to ikat, *kasuri* is a resist-dye method whereby the threads
are tightly bound before weaving and immersed in dye. The design
emerges as the cloth is woven. This technique was mostly used with
indigo-dyed cotton and bast fibres (*asa*), however, this example is made
of silk, suggesting it was made after the abolishment of sumptuary laws
in the late 19th century. It features sewn-on ties, making it easier for
the parent to dress their child and is slightly wadded for added comfort.
The techniques of ikat patterning were introduced to Japan via the
Ryūkyū Islands, the archipelago to the south-west of Honshū, which
was part of a thriving maritime trade network within Asia.

An intricate network of diamonds decorate the back and neckline of this robe, making it the central feature of focus on an otherwise plain garment. This needlework technique is known as *kogin*. Executed in white cotton on an indigo-dyed plain-weave bast-fibre (*asa*) ground, *kogin* originates in the Tsugaru region at the northern part of mainland Japan (Honshū). The loose weave of the bast fibre makes it easy to count the warp threads when creating this complex geometric pattern. Unlike many other garments in the collection, this would have been made by the person who wore it, possibly for her wedding day. The ability to weave and embroider were important skills for women of this region with most learning from childhood.

Robe for a woman
Plain-weave bast fibre (*asa*);
stitched cotton design (*kogin*)
1880–1920

FE.141-198

Parading Courtesan
Katsukawa Shunsen (1762–1830)
Colour print from woodblocks
Edo (Tokyo), 1804–18

E.12564-1886

**Kimono for a young woman
(*furisode*)**
Figured silk satin (*rinzu*); tie-dyeing
(*shibori*)
Probably Kyoto, 1800–40

FE.32-1982

Kimono are straight seamed garments worn with the left side
wrapped over the right, producing a V-shape at the neck.
This kimono would have been worn by a young, unmarried woman.
It has an overall hemp-leaf (*asa no ha*) design dyed on silk woven with
a small key-fret and flower pattern (*sayagata*). The collar, hem and
sleeves feature roundels with the auspicious motifs of plum blossom,
bamboo and pine. These plants are known in Japan as the 'three friends
of winter' (*shochikubai*) and frequently feature in kimono design. The
plum tree is the first to blossom after winter and together with the
evergreen bamboo and pine symbolize longevity, perseverance and
renewal. This pattern has been created using *shibori*, a labour-intensive
tie-dye technique whereby small sections of the cloth are bound before
being submerged in dye. Safflower, an expensive dye known as *beni*
in Japanese, was used to produce this distinctive red. Although vibrant,
the colour can easily fade and is thus associated with the fleeting
experiences of youth and passion.

Kimono for a woman (*hōmongi*)
Figured silk satin (*rinzu*); gold leaf and
embroidery in metallic thread (kimono)
Polychrome figured silk (*obi*)
c. 1960

Given anonymously
FE.74-2012; FE.75-2012

This semi-formal garment is a style known as a *hōmongi*. They are
typically decorated in a way known as *eba* where the design sweeps
over the seams. A rich purple diamond motif sits slightly off centre on
the back of this elegant kimono. Below to the right is a chrysanthemum
richly embroidered in gold wrapped thread. Such patterns require
the artisan to draw the design, which is often asymmetric, while the
kimono is temporarily sewn together and then taken apart to be
decorated. Once it has been dyed and embroidered, most likely in
separate workshops, it is sewn back together into a kimono. Each step
is yet another layer of luxury. This ensemble, which includes the gold
obi pictured here and the vermilion *obi* featured on p. 123, was a gift
from the daughter of the emperor of Japan to a member of the British
royal family. The technical sophistication, lavish use of applied gold leaf,
and chrysanthemums and paulownia motifs – emblems of the Japanese
imperial family and government respectively – are entirely appropriate
for such an important diplomatic gift.

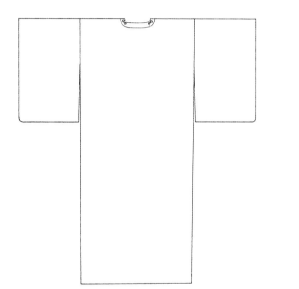
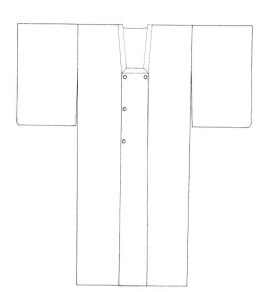

Coat for a woman (*michiyuki*)
Figured silk gauze (*ra*)
Kyoto, 1993–5
Kitamura Takeshi
FE.274-1995

This three-quarter length coat is a *michiyuki*, which literally means 'while on the road'. This style of woman's outer garment developed in the 20th century. It has a low, square neckline, designed to reveal the kimono that would be worn underneath and is fastened with six press-studs. Four fabric-covered buttons are sewn onto the front. The coat was created by Kitamura Takeshi (b. 1935) who has studied and recreated one of the earliest, and most sophisticated, Japanese gauze-weaving techniques. It has a lattice pattern woven from silk thread, which was dyed before weaving with a vegetable dye derived from pomegranates. The fabric was woven in 1993 and made up into a *michiyuki* especially for the Victoria and Albert Museum in 1995, the same year that Kitamura was awarded the prestigious title of Living National Treasure.

Kimono for a man (kosode)
Figured silk satin (*rinzu*)
Probably Kyoto, 1760–1810

Given by Yoshida Kōjirō
FE.201-2018

Marked with the crest (*mon*) of the Nabeshima clan on a checkerboard ground, this kimono is believed to have belonged to the lord (*daimyō*) of this powerful Samurai family who ruled the Saga Domain on the island of Kyūshū in south-west Japan. In comparison to women's garments, men's kimono were relatively plain. However, luxurious fabrics with subtle decoration were what marked out the dress for men of such high rank. It was probably worn with a *hakama*, a pleated lower garment. This is one of the earliest examples of men's dress from Japan.

A white dress shirt and burgundy silk necktie transform this kimono into business attire. The navy pinstripe fabric is by John Foster, a British company founded in 1819 that specializes in textiles for suits and won the first prize for alpaca and mohair fabrics at London's Great Exhibition of 1851. However, the ensemble is by Fujikiya, a Japanese brand specializing in men's kimono. Fujikiya's designer, Kidera Masaru (b. 1980), started out as a tailor, but has made it his mission to encourage more men to wear kimono by offering a made-to-measure service and range of practical fabrics, including denim. In a culture where corporate life is the focus for many men, the suit kimono is an ingenious development in Japanese dress.

Kimono with shirt and necktie for a man
Worsted wool (kimono); plain-weave cotton (shirt); polychrome figured silk (*obi* and necktie)
Tokyo, 2018

Fujikiya (fabric by John Foster)

FE.278 to 290-2018

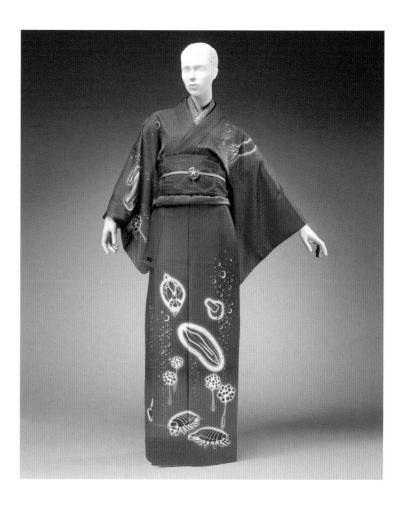

Kimono for a woman with half collar (*han-eri*)
Digitally printed polyester; braided silk; resin; starfish
Tokyo, 2016

Iroca

FE.32 to 36-2018

Kimono are worn in layers that would often create visual contrast at the neck. Today most are worn with plain white collars; however, decorative half-collars (*han-eri*) are often added to enhance the kimono ensemble. Formed of a small rectangular length of fabric, these are sewn to the collars of under kimono (*naga-juban*). Small sections of this brightly coloured *han-eri* are visible below an equally bold kimono. Made of teal polyester crêpe, it has a psychedelic design of fluorescent mushrooms that harmonizes with the vibrant underwater patterns on the kimono and *obi*. All of these pieces are by Iroca, a kimono brand based in Tokyo. Founded by Ishikawa Narutoshi (b. 1965) in 2001, the brand started with accessories rather than kimono. For Ishikawa, all aspects of Japanese dress need to reflect contemporary design, an ambition achieved through his vivid use of colour and imaginative patterns which are digitally printed on polyester.

Hat (*takuhatsu-gasa*)
Woven straw
1950–2012

Given by Rev. Zenkō Croysdale
FE.100-2012

Wide-brimmed hats such as this are called *takuhatsu-gasa* and are worn by Buddhist monks. Based on the historic travelling dress of pilgrims, they are designed so that the brim covers the face. A bamboo support within fits to the crown of the head, ensuring the hat is secure. Such hats are worn when collecting alms, a practice known in Zen Buddhism as *takuhatsu* after which they are named. This practice, in which lay people offer food and money, is thought to embody Zen virtues of humility and gratitude.

Headdress (*kanmuri*)
Silk gauze, stiffened and lacquered;
paper-string
1800–1900

T.518:1-1919

This ceremonial headdress is a style known as a
kanmuri and was worn by officials of the ceremonial
court, Shinto priests or *Nō* actors playing these roles.
Made of delicate, stiffened silk gauze, this headdress
epitomizes refined court culture. It consists of a
skull-cap, vertical section and pin, and tail section,
known as an *ei*, that trails down the back of the wearer
and signifies rank. Although made in the 19th century,
the style itself has changed little since it was first
developed in the Heian period (794–1185). *Kanmuri*
thus served as a symbol of these romanticized times
and were sometimes used as a motif on kimono to
evoke courtly scenes.

Firefighter's hood and jacket
Quilted plain-weave cotton (*sashiko*);
freehand resist-dyed decoration
(*tsutsugaki*)
1850–1900

FE.107A-1982

This hood, along with its matching jacket, would have been worn by an urban firefighter in the late 19th century. It is made from several layers of thick indigo-blue cotton quilted together using a technique called *sashiko*. A dynamic resist-dyed pattern of stormy clouds, rain and red bolts of lightning decorate the lining, and the ties have contrasting horizontal and vertical geometric bands. Long flaps at either side and at the back serve to protect the face and neck, while the crown is heavily padded in case of falling debris. Before tackling a blaze, the firefighter would pull down the side flaps in order to be drenched in water to guard himself against the flames; the layers of cloth on the hood and jacket allowed for maximum absorption. Fire was rife in densely populated cities where most of the buildings were constructed of wood.

Lacquered gold leather and richly embroidered jewel-toned wool are unlikely materials for a firefighter's hood. This particular style would have belonged to a woman of the samurai class who would not have actively battled flames. The outer red layer has the family crest (*mon*), possibly of the Honda clan, and is edged with butterflies, while the purple underlayer has an autumnal motif of chrysanthemums among bamboo fencing embroidered in white, pink and green floss silk and couched gold. Three bands of silk crêpe in red, white and purple run along the base of the leather section, forming a bow at the back fastened by a gilt-edged ornament in the form of a chrysanthemum, the ends trailing down the back.

Firefighter's hood
Lacquered leather; silk crêpe; felted wool (*rasha*); embroidery in silk and metallic threads
1850–1900

T.64-1909

Comb
Wood with red-, gold-, silver- and
black-sprinkled lacquer (*hiramaki-e*)
and inlaid shell (*raden*)
1800–1900

Signed Eiho

Given by Fumie Kosuge
FE.21-2002

Most dress accessories are made by anonymous artisans, however, this
comb has been signed 'Eiho', signifying that this was a maker of repute.
The deep red ground, created by adding the powdered mineral pigment
to clear lacquer, provides an ideal surface for the richly textured
decoration of a golden peony and other flora. In addition to sprinkled
metallic powder, small pieces of shell have been inlaid into the flowers
to provide extra sparkle. Such details, although small, would catch the
light and make a highly attractive impression.

Comb
Wood with carved polychrome lacquer
1850–1900

Signed Kochō

Given by Fumie Kosuge
FE.24-2002

A strikingly modern pattern of raindrops has been formed by carving
away small sections on the surface of this comb, revealing layers of
red-and-green coloured lacquer below the black-lacquer top coats.
Framed by gold, the predominant use of black lacquer would have made
this an incredibly subtle ornament when worn in dark hair. As Japanese
dress is not worn with jewellery, hair accessories such as this provided
the principal form of ornament for women.

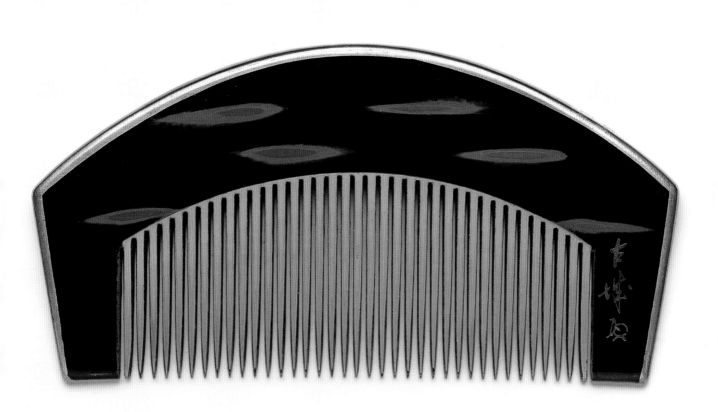

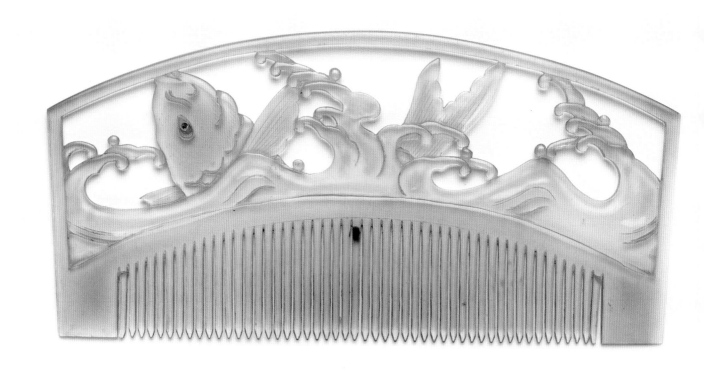

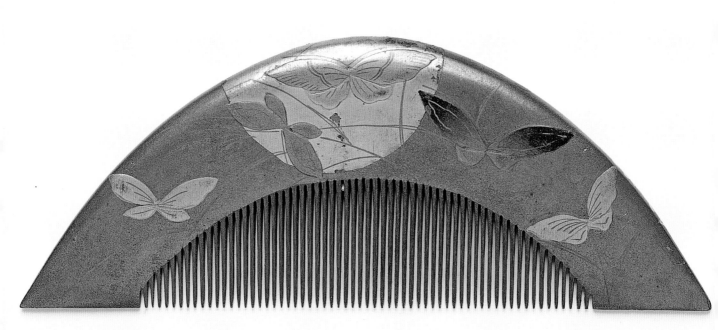

A carp flexes in turbulent water on this delicate tortoiseshell comb. The openwork carved scene on this comb skilfully conveys a sense of depth and drama. Such stylized waves are reminiscent of Katsushika Hokusai's print, *In the Hollow of a Wave off the Coast at Kanagawa* (*The Great Wave*) from the series *Thirty-six Views of Mount Fuji*. While this is not directly based on one of his design, Hokusai did create designs for hair combs, sometimes adapting elements from his prints to the form of this fashion accessory.

Comb
Blond tortoiseshell carved in openwork
1850–88
84-1888

BELOW
Oshichi of the Yaoya House
Kitagawa Utamaro (1753–1806)
Colour print from woodblocks
Edo (Tokyo), c. 1800
E.427-1895

This elegant semi-circular comb is decorated on both sides with an autumnal scene of moths and grasses with a full moon behind. Made of wood covered in silver lacquer, the design has been applied by sprinkling on gold-, silver- and black-coloured powders into wet lacquer, a technique known as *hiramaki-e* ('low-sprinkled picture'). When worn in the hair, the silver comb resembled a crescent moon.

Comb
Wood with gold-, silver- and black-sprinkled lacquer (*hiramaki-e*)
1850–88
43-1888

The Courtesan Yosooi
of the Matsuba-ya
Chokosai Eishō (active 1790–1800)
Colour print from woodblocks
Edo (Tokyo), 1790s

Given by the Misses Alexander
E.1414-1898

Comb and hairpins
Carved wood and lacquer inlaid
with gold foil (*kirikane*); shell (*raden*)
1900–25

Given by Fumie Kosuge
FE.60-2002; FE.61-2002; FE.62-2002

Tiny pieces of shell create natural glitter on this glamorous comb
and matching hairpins. The design of chrysanthemums, plum blossom
and bamboo has been carved into the wood with some decoration
continuing over to the top of the teeth. Different shades of shell – each
piece expertly cut by hand and colour-graded – have been used, with
pink and yellow for the flowers and green for the background. The
hirauchi-style hairpin with a circular design at the head incorporates
tortoiseshell and has a motif of paulownia leaves.

Courtesan Hanaogi of Ogi-ya
Utagawa Kunisada (1786–1864)
Colour print from woodblocks
c. 1830

E.1371-1899

Combs
Wood with gold and silver *hiramaki-e*
and *togidashi maki-e* lacquer
1800–80

38-1888

Wood with black lacquer inlaid with
copper, *shibuichi* and mother-of-pearl
1850–1900

Given by Fumie Kosuge
FE.34-2002

Wood with black, gold and silver
lacquer inlaid with *aogai* shell
Biho
1850–1900

Given by Fumie Kosuge
FE.26-2002

Tortoiseshell inlaid with coloured ivory,
shell and metal
1800–1900

Given by Fumie Kosuge
FE.18-2002

Hairpins and hair ornament
Tortoiseshell and wood with black
lacquer inlaid with mother-of-pearl,
silver and metal; tortoiseshell, carved,
incised and inlaid with hardstones
and silver; wood with black lacquer
inlaid with shell; tortoiseshell; silver
and black lacquer
1850–1900

Given by Fumie Kosuge
FE.32-2002; FE.42-2002; FE.13-2002;
FE.10-2002; FE.15-2002

As hairstyles became larger and more complicated during the Edo
period, greater importance was placed on hair accessories (*kanzashi*).
While combs were worn by most women in society, it was hairpins that
became an essential feature of fashion. There are a range of various
styles of *kanzashi*, which are made in a variety of materials including
lacquer, tortoiseshell, ivory, metal and fabric. The most lavish *kanzashi*
incorporated precious stones while more humble examples were plain
wood or paper. Famous courtesans wore an elaborate array of *kanzashi*
as a marker of status and to attract attention, as seen in prints such
as this example by Utagawa Kunisada that depicts Hanaogi of Ogi-ya.

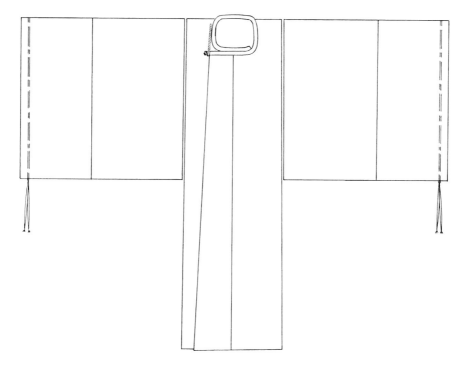

Court robe for a man (*kariginu*)
Figured silk gauze
Probably Kyoto, 1850–1900

FE.157-1983

Japanese robes are differentiated by their style of sleeve. Those with small openings at the wrist are known as *kosode* (pp. 48, 79 and 98), while robes such as this, with a wide wrist opening that extends along the entire width of the sleeve, are called *ōsode*. This kind of large, loose sleeve allows for a layered look, the edges of the garments worn underneath being attractively revealed. Voluminous *ōsode*, made of stiff, woven fabrics, are worn at the imperial court. This garment is a *kariginu* (hunting cloak). To allow for maximum ease of movement when drawing a bow on horseback, the double width sleeves are attached to the body of the garment only at the upper back and the cords threaded along the cuffs allow the sleeve to be gathered up. This example was made in the second half of the 19th century, by which time *kariginu* were no longer worn for hunting but as part of the everyday costumes of court nobles. It is a summer garment, the open structure of the gauze making it perfect for hot, humid weather. Worn over other robes, the transparency of the cloth would have created a shimmering effect.

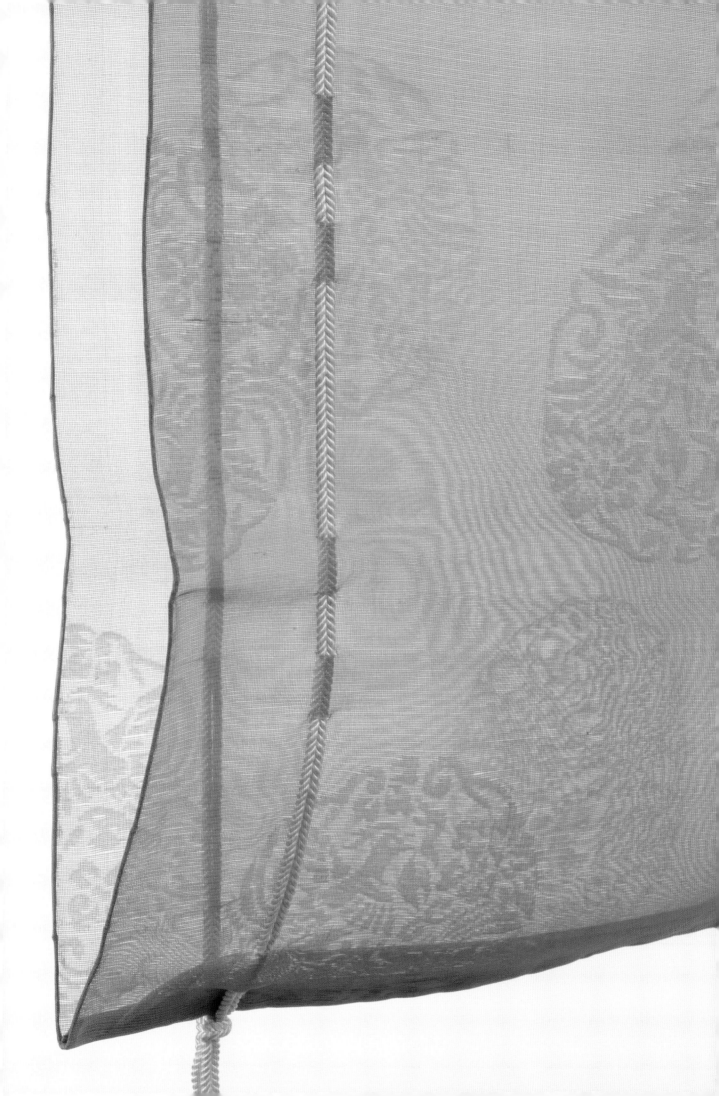

Outer kimono for a woman (*uchikake*)

Plain-weave silk crêpe (*chirimen*); freehand paste resist-dyeing (*yūzen*); embroidery in silk and metallic threads
Probably Kyoto, 1750–1800

Given by Mrs Sydney Avis
T.64-1954

While young, unmarried women wear long, fluttering sleeves (*furisode*), married women are required to wear shorter sleeves such as these that feature on this kimono. The padded hem indicates that the garment is an outer kimono, for winter wear, while the small-scale pattern suggests that it was made in the mid-18th century. The delicate design of flowers, birds and butterflies at the water's edge was created using a resist-dyeing technique known as *yūzen*. This involves drawing the pattern on the cloth with rice paste extruded through the metal tip of a cloth bag. The paste forms a protective coat that prevents the colour penetrating when the dyes are applied. Touches of embroidery in red, green and couched gold provide added contrast against the blue ground that represents a clear sky (*asagi*).

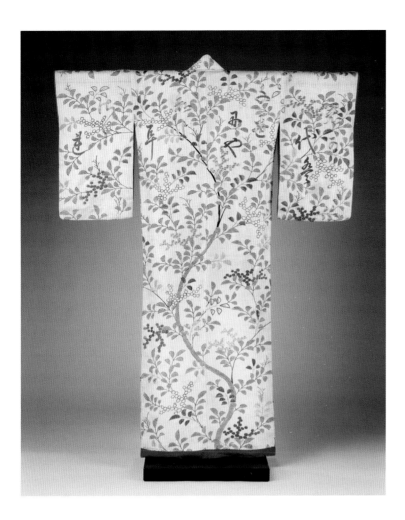

One of the most common types of Japanese dress is known as *kosode*. Rather than length, the term refers to size of the sleeve opening, which is small in comparison to the courtly *ōsode* (p. 74). The sleeves and shoulders of this elegant *kosode* are decorated with calligraphic characters, indicating the wearer's literary inclinations. Designed to be read from right to left, the first characters are on this sleeve and read '*kimi*' and '*yo*', probably a reference to a Heian poem from the anthology *Kokin Wakashūshu*. It was from this that the Japanese national anthem 'Kimigayo' was later adapted during the Meiji period. As with the leaves and berries of the nandina tree that form most of the pattern, the characters are embroidered in polychrome floss silk and couched gold wrapped thread. Additional decorative techniques used are stencil imitation tie-dyeing (*suri-hitta*) and ink painting applied directly onto the cloth by hand. The white ground is woven with a pattern of key-fret and small flower design known as *sayagata*, adding depth and an extra layer of luxury to what is a highly sophisticated garment.

Kimono for a woman (*kosode*)
Figured silk satin (*rinzu*) with ink painting (*kaki-e*); stencil imitation tie-dyeing (*suri-hitta*); embroidery in silk and metallic threads
Probably Kyoto, 1780–1820

FE.19-1986

**Kimono for a young woman
(*furisode*)**
Plain-weave silk crêpe (*chirimen*);
tie-dyeing (*shibori*); embroidery
in silk and metallic threads
Probably Kyoto, 1900–30

FE.17-1984

This striking kimono is called a *furisode*, literally 'swinging sleeves',
denoting the long lengths of fabric that hang below the arm. This style
of garment was worn by young, unmarried women. The five crests are
a feature of formal wear. Various decorative techniques have been used
to create the dramatic pattern. Small-scale tie-dyeing (*kanoko shibori*)
has been used to form the bamboo that is partially obscured by
atmospheric clouds, which are also tie-dyed (*shibori*), and then scored
with gold. Exuberant plum blossoms embroidered in both polychrome
silk and couched gold-wrapped thread are overlaid on top. Such a
glamorous garment would have been worn by a highly fashionable
young woman keen to enhance her beauty and attract attention.

Long sleeves (*furisode*) are a feature of bridal kimono. This kimono was probably made for a wedding and is a style that continues to be worn by brides today (p. 157). The shimmering white ground of figured silk satin (*rinzu*) has a distinctive pattern of sinuous lines representing rising mist (*tatewaku*) bordering botanical motifs. Captivating glimpses of the red silk-crêpe lining can be seen at the sleeve openings. The sleeves are embroidered to correspond with the overall decoration. On the lower part, chrysanthemums of orange, yellow, green and brown silk grow up fences couched in gold thread. Above are butterflies in similar colours, no two of which are the same.

Outer kimono for a young woman (*furisode uchikake*)
Figured silk satin (*rinzu*); embroidery in silk and metallic threads
Probably Kyoto, 1840–70

Given by Mrs Mockett
T.269-1960

Robe
Plain-weave cotton with stencilled
decoration (*bingata*)
Shuri, 1850–1900

T.18-1963

While having some similarities to the structure of kimono, the sleeves
of Ryūkyūan garments are attached to the body of the garment
and left fully open. This striking pattern of cranes, pine trees, clouds
and chrysanthemums has been created using a Ryūkyūan technique
known as *bingata* that employs stencils and bright mineral pigments.
This robe was made and worn in Okinawa, the largest of the islands
in the Ryūkyūan archipelago that stretches to the south of mainland
Japan. The islands were an independent kingdom until 1879 when they
became part of Japan. Robes such as this were worn only by members
of the Ryūkyūan royal family.

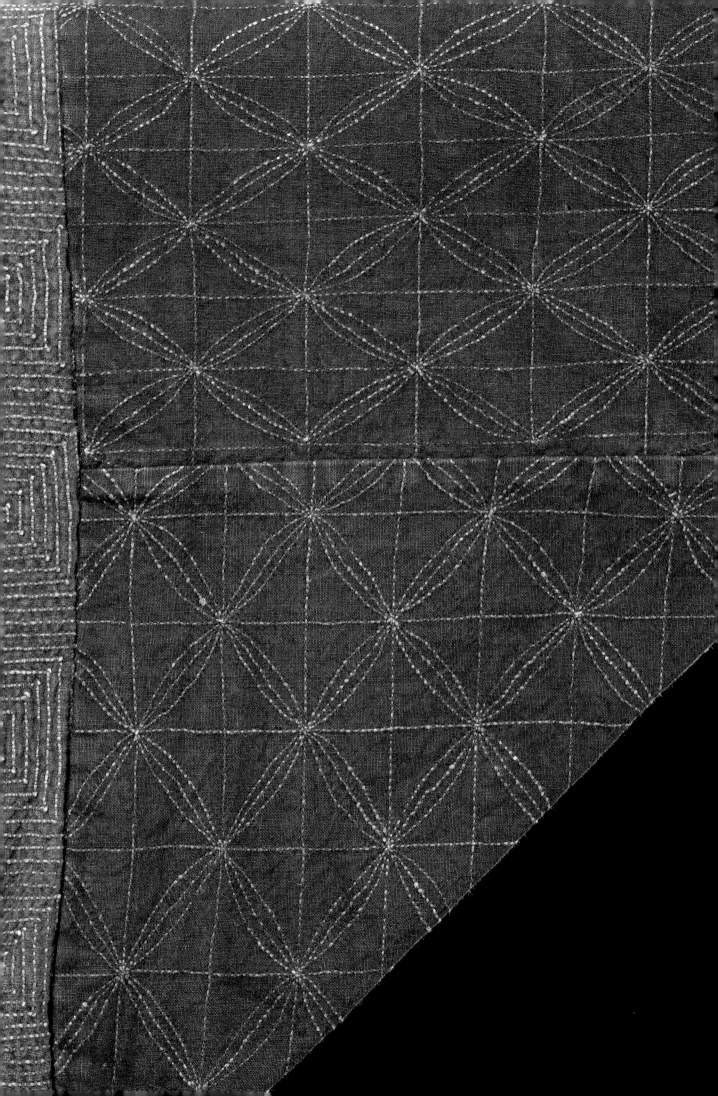

Tapered sleeves such as this are typical features of work clothing.
The diagonal seams allow for freedom of movement and do not need
to be tied back, as square sleeves often are for housework. This robe is
made from two layers of cotton, deeply dyed with indigo so as to appear
black, which have been stitched together with lighter blue thread using
a quilting technique known as *sashiko*. A variety of stitches have been
employed on different parts of the garment. Interlocking curvilinear
lattice designs pattern the sleeves, while the main body of the garment
features *masu zashi* (stacking boxes) and the nape of the neck is densely
stitched with a diamond pattern. *Sashiko* cotton was popular throughout
the country, but was a particularly important technique in northern
Japan where it provided much needed warmth and insulation in the
colder climate.

Coat for a farmer
Plain-weave cotton; quilted (*sashiko*)
1850–1900

FE.30-1982

Sophisticated tie-dyeing (*shibori*) creates the distinctive form of Mount Fuji on the sleeve of this dramatic kimono. Made from hemp, a fibre that has long been valued for its suitability to the Japanese climate, this garment was created by Yamaguchi Genbei (b. 1948) as part of the Majotae Project, which aims to produce hemp cloth (*taima-fu*) on a sufficiently large scale to make it commercially viable for clothing manufacture. A keen researcher of historic techniques, Genbei is the tenth-generation head of Kyoto-based *obi* purveyor Kondaya Genbei and regularly collaborates with the most talented artisans as well as contemporary artists and designers.

Kimono for a woman
Machine-spun hemp (*taima-fu*), tie-dyeing (*shibori*)
Kyoto, 2019

Yamaguchi Genbei for the Majotae Project

FE.126-2019

Robe for *Nō* theatre (*atsuita*)
Polychrome figured silk
Probably Kyoto, 1750–1850

Given by Mrs Edmund de Rothschild
T.297-1963

Dragons and stylized clouds on a ground of interlocking triangles, a pattern that represents scales (*uroko*), adorn this striking robe. The bold design, which appears to be embroidered, is actually created with a highly sophisticated three-layered weaving technique. *Atsuita* were worn by actors playing dominant male roles such as warlords, gods or demons and have geometric patterns with masculine motifs such as dragons. Despite the lavish fabric, most of the garment would have been covered by an outer *kariginu* robe. The name for this style of costume, *atsuita,* derives from the luxurious Chinese textiles from which they were first made. These bolts of cloth were rolled around thick wooden boards (*atsu-ita*) when imported to Japan. Costumes for *Nō* theatre are some of the most exceptional examples of Japanese dress, many being commissioned by the high-ranking samurai who sponsored acting troupes.

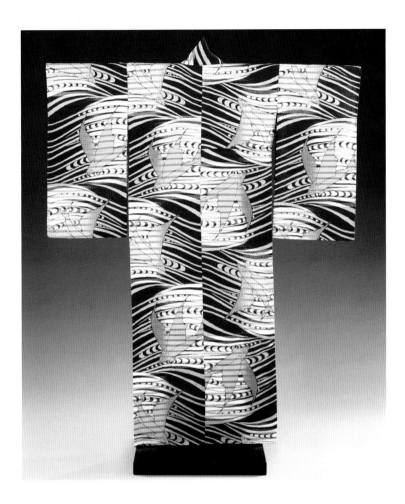

Many informal kimono from the early 20th century have longer sleeves, suggesting that these were items of fashion, rather than practical garments. The repeat pattern of flying fish and stylized waves in purple, yellow, blue and white with hints of silver was typical of the bold style popular at the time. It was made using what was a new and inexpensive technique known as *meisen*. This process uses machine-spun silk and aniline dyes, the latter mixed with rice paste and applied to the warp before weaving through stencils, to create modern and dynamic patterns. *Meisen* kimono were favoured by urban young women keen to participate in contemporary fashion during a period of rapid change. Despite the decline in casual kimono wearing following the Second World War, *meisen* production managed to survive in areas such as Isesaki and is currently enjoying a revival.

Summer kimono for a woman (*hitoe*)
Machine-spun plain-weave pongee silk; stencil dyeing of warp and weft (heiyō-gasuri) and supplementary silver wefts
Probably Isesaki, 1920–40

FE.47-2014

Kimono for a child
Plain-weave wool; printed
1937
FE.2-2005

By the 20th century children's clothing tended to be more comfortable and functional, rather than being miniature versions of adult dress. This has been achieved here through various features, such as the slanted sleeve, plain-weave wool, soft wadding and two long ties at the front. The pattern celebrates the first flight from Tokyo to London in 1937. Featured within this graphic print is a globe that notes the various stops the plane, called the Kamikaze-gō, made before landing at Croydon, near London on 9 April. Icons of Japan and Britain – Mount Fuji and Tower Bridge respectively – also feature in the design, as do the flags of France and the UK. Although made at a time of fervent nationalism, the term '*kamikaze*' does not refer to the Japanese Special Attack Units of the Second World War, merely the name of the Japanese-built aircraft, the literal translation being 'divine wind'.

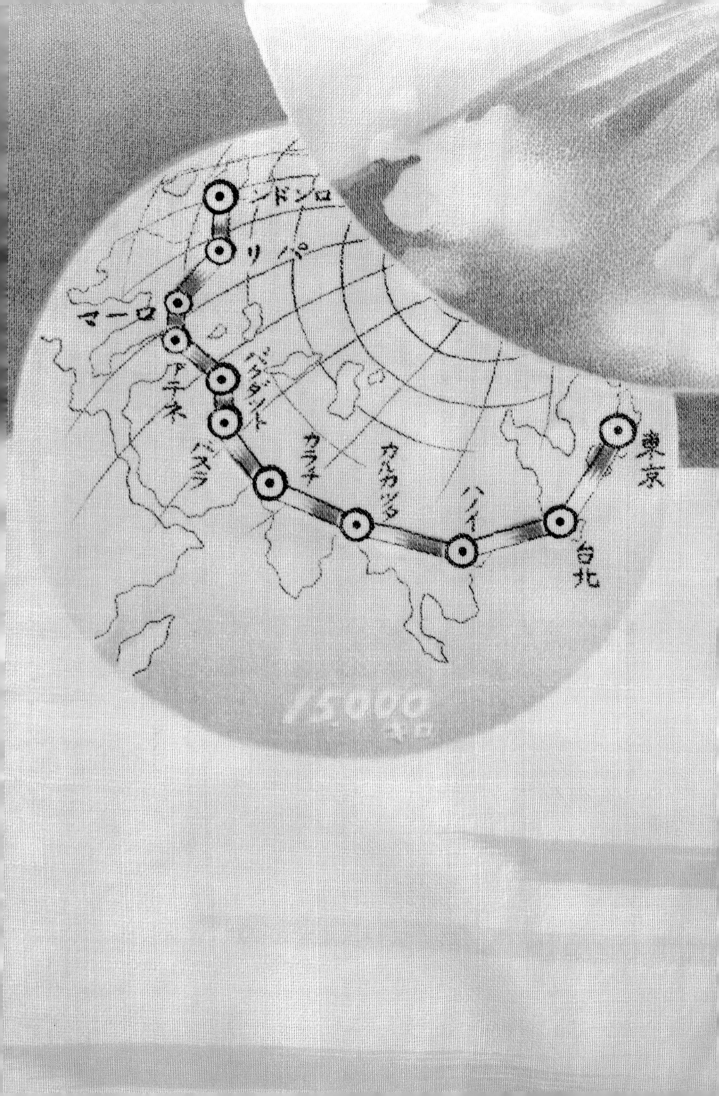

The design by Shigemune Tamao (b. 1981) makes full use of the long sleeves on this *furisode* (swinging-sleeve) kimono. At the front a pair of swans grace each sleeve, surrounded by pink, white and yellow roses, butterflies and bumble bees with a large red and white striped ribbon at the right shoulder. The Surrealist-inspired design is digitally printed on a figured silk (*rinzu*) woven with a dotted pattern. Entitled *Engagement Ribbon*, Shigemune created this kimono after her own marriage proposal. While her brand is based in Tokyo, this kimono was made at the Kyoto studio of fellow contemporary kimono makers Modern Antenna. Formal kimono such as *furisode* are usually rather conventional, making this an exceptional piece.

Kimono for a young woman (*furisode*)
Figured silk; digitally printed
Kyoto, 2016

Shigemune Tamao

FE.43-2018

Kimono for a man (*kosode*)
Brocade silk (*nishiki*)
Probably Kyoto, 1860–90

Given by T.B. Clarke-Thornhill
T.65-1915

A fish jumping through water decorates this unusual kimono that once belonged to kabuki actor Ichikawa Danjūrō IX. The auspicious motif relates to a legend in which fish that are able to leap over a mighty waterfall are transformed into dragons. The story is a metaphor for male achievement and advancement. Kabuki actors were the fashion leaders of the Edo period, however, it is not known whether the garment was worn for performance or off-stage.

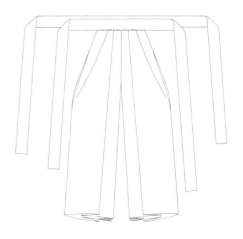

Pair of trousers for a man (*sashinuki*)
Polychrome figured twill silk (*mon aya*)
Probably Kyoto, 1800–80

Given by T.B. Clark-Thornhill
T.68-1915

Pleated *hakama*, variously described as full-cut trousers or a divided skirt, were an important item of dress for both men and women of the Japanese imperial court and men of the samurai class. *Hakama* are wide with broad pleats and taper towards the top, being secured with bands that wrap and tie around the waist. The sides are open halfway down, revealing the robes worn underneath. This example is of a type known as *sashinuki*, which would have been worn tied tight around the hems so that the excess fabric would have ballooned out over the ankles. *Sashinuki* were worn by court nobles.

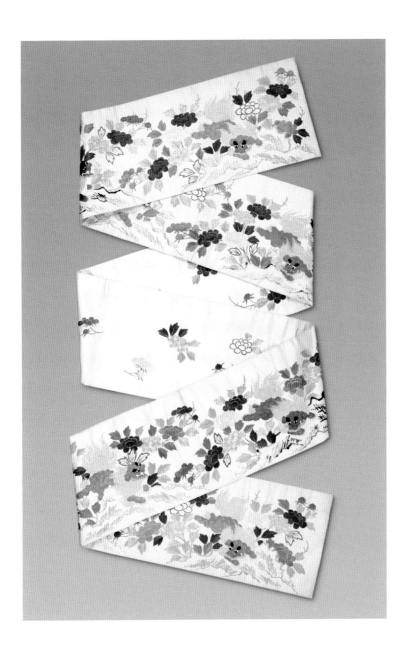

Animated *shishi* (mythical lions) among peonies decorate the length of this sumptuous satin *obi*. An expert range of stitches is employed to depict these fabled creatures: clusters of knot stitches (*sagara-nui*) are used for the mane, the fur is made of a combination of long and short stitches (*sashi-nui*) while the prominent eyebrows are knotted and cut to create pile. In contrast, long, untwisted floss silk has been used for the flowers. The combination of *shishi* with peonies is an auspicious motif associated with the play *Shakkyō* (*The Stone Bridge*). The story tells of a monk, Jakushō, who visits Mount Shōryōzen in China where he finds a long, narrow bridge over a deep gorge, which is reputed to lead to the Pure Land and where *shishi* dance surrounded by peonies. Historic *obi* rarely survive as the strain from tying them weakens the fabric making them more vulnerable to damage.

Obi for a woman

Silk satin (*shusu*); embroidery in silk and metallic threads
Probably Kyoto, 1850–70

Given by Mrs Mockett
T.270-1960

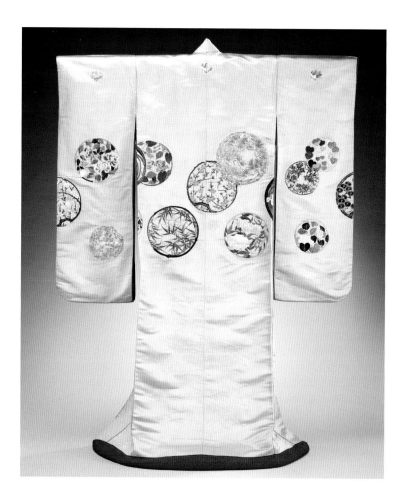

Outer kimono for a woman (uchikake)
Silk satin (*shusu*); embroidery in silk and metallic threads
Probably Kyoto, 1800–50

FE.11-1983

Delicate roundels of flowers and foliage of the four seasons adorn the waist of this outer kimono (*uchikake*). The highly sophisticated embroidery employs a variety of stitches to depict an array of motifs including plum blossom, peonies, irises, hydrangeas, pine and bamboo. The roundels, which sometimes overlap each other and sometimes appear singly, are mostly embroidered in polychrome floss silk in satin stitch and its variation long and short stitch while some, including the five crests, are couched in gold-wrapped threads. As the waist area is usually covered by the *obi*, many kimono are plain in the middle section. However, *uchikake* are winter garments designed to be worn unsecured over kimono and *obi*. This elegant garment was probably made for a woman of samurai class for a special occasion, perhaps her wedding ceremony.

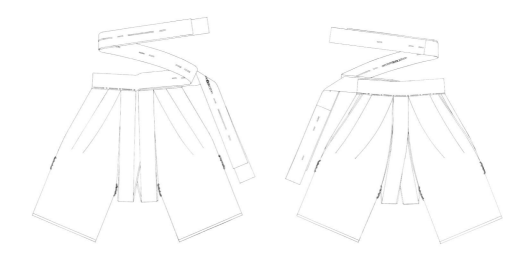

Pair of trousers for a man (*hakama*)
Figured twill silk (*mon aya*); silk lining;
silk cord
Probably Kyoto, 1800–80

Given by T.B. Clark-Thornhill
T.66-1915

The formal costume for male members of the Japanese court is known as *sokutai* and consists of various layers of long upper garments, or *hō*, and two pairs of *hakama*. This is a pair of outer *hakama*, woven in white silk with roundels of wisteria. The red silk lining is revealed at the side openings, hems, along the bands and on the two broad loops that conceal the opening at the crotch. White, laced double cords reinforce the top of the side seams, and pairs of cords, elaborately knotted at intervals, decorate the long waist bands.

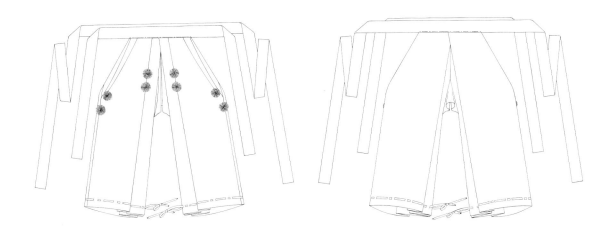

Blue-and-white pompom-like knots adorn this pair of *hakama*.
They would have been worn by a samurai. The knots would have
originally helped to reinforce the seams, but by the 19th century
when this garment was made, they were more decorative than
functional. The matching jacket and trouser ensemble is known as
a *hitatare*. This particular two-piece outfit may have been designed
to wear under armour, the braids at the hem allowing the trousers
to be gathered up and tucked into boots. The Edo period was a time
of peace in Japan so there was no opportunity for samurai to engage
in actual warfare. However, armour would still be worn on ceremonial
occasions and when provincial lords marched with their retinue in
procession to and from the capital. *Hitatare* were made from rich and
elaborately woven fabrics designed to emphasize the samurai's status
and enhance the dramatic effect of the whole outfit.

Pair of trousers for a man (*hakama*)
Polychrome figured twill silk (*mon aya*)
Probably Kyoto, 1800–50

79-1890

Obi for a woman

Silk velvet; embroidery in silk
and metallic threads
Probably Kyoto, 1850–70

Given by Mrs J. Douglas Watson
FE.23-1973

Made of silk velvet and richly embroidered on both sides, this *obi* is
the height of luxurious dress. Scattered circular and lozenge-shaped
cartwheels rest among peonies, wisteria and wild ginger in shades of
green, orange, purple and gold metallic thread on a rich yellow ground.
Various stiches have been employed to provide texture and detail
including flat stitch (*hira-nui*), knot stitch (*sagara-nui*) and threads held
down within lattice stitching (*goban-osae*) together with gold-wrapped
threads couched onto the surface. It was during the Edo period that
obi became prominent parts of Japanese dress, often considered of
equal status to kimono particularly when richly decorated like this
example. While the style suggests an Edo period date, the vivid purple
thread appears to be made from aniline dye, making it very late Edo
or even Meiji period.

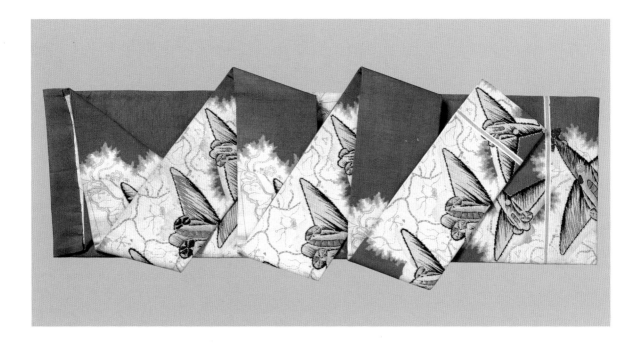

Obi for a woman
Plain-weave silk; stencil dyed (*kata-yūzen*);
embroidery in silk and metallic threads
1930–40s

FE.46-2014

Created with stencils printed on the fabric surface (*kata-yūzen*), the distinctive repeat pattern on this *obi* consists of warplanes flying over a topographical map of China. The planes have been further embellished in places with embroidery in silk and metallic threads. Geographic details such as the Great Wall and the names of various cities – Shanghai, Nanjing, Qingdao, Jinan, Beijing and Rehe – allude to Japan's colonial ambitions on the mainland. During the Second World War many people wore propaganda designs to display their nationalism. Although more commonly found on under kimono (*naga-juban*) for men and boys (see pp. 16 and 169), this *obi* shows women would sometimes publicly proclaim patriotism through their dress.

**Obi and obi-cord for a woman
(kakae-obi, obi-jime)**
Polychrome figured silk
1934
Retailed by Shirokiya

Given by Kōji Shimojima
FE.139.1, 2-2002

**Wedding of Shimojima Saburō
and Sachiko**
Photograph
Tokyo, 1934

These kimono accessories, *kakae-obi* and matching *obi-jime*, were part of a wedding ensemble. *Kakae-obi* are thin sashes worn below the *obi* for formal wear, such as bridal kimono, while the padded *obi-jime* helps to secure the knot and is worn at the middle of the *obi*. Woven with supplementary wefts of gold-gilt paper strips (*kinran*) on a red ground, the repeat pattern of cranes and flowers within interlocking octagons is suitably auspicious. Cranes symbolize longevity and are popular motifs for bridal garments. These were worn by Shimojima Sachiko on her wedding day on 1 February 1934 (above, right).

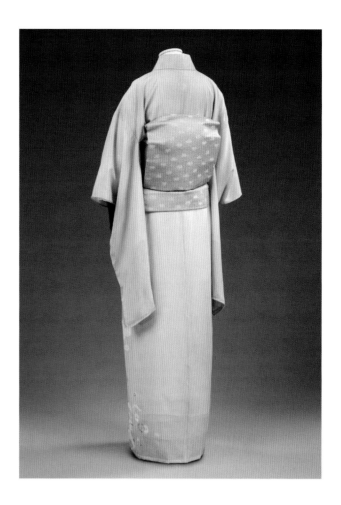

Obi for a woman
Figured twill silk
1950s

Given by Sarah Brooks in memory of
her mother Bernice Eileen (Wiese) Boo
FE.36:1, 2-2015

Following the Second World War, the number of people wearing
kimono reduced drastically. In turn, the ability to wear a kimono and
tie an *obi* went from being tacit knowledge to a rare skill. Producers
of Japanese dress quickly responded by developing easy options, such
as this pre-tied *obi* (*tsuke-obi*). It is made from two pieces; a short sash
with cotton cords to tie in simple knot and a decorative bow in the form
of a drum knot (*taiko musabi*) with hooks that attach to the sash when
secured. This *obi* is made of a twill-weave green ground with white
supplementary wefts forming a pattern of maple leaves and stylized
waves. The colour and autumnal motifs correspond directly with the
kimono, an unlined summer style of gauze weave (*ro*). It is unusual for
a kimono and *obi* to be matched, especially in such a uniform way,
as a level of contrast is usually desired. This style of *obi* was a popular
gift to foreigners visiting Japan, which was presumably how the owner,
Bernice Eileen (Wiese) Boo, acquired it. She taught at the Narimasu
High School, Grant Heights, Tokyo, from 1957 to 1959.

Obi for a woman
Polychrome figured silk
1960–80

Given by Janice Thorburn
FE.58-2015

An idealized landscape of boats and thatched cottages on a lake with mountains rising above clouds decorates this *obi*. Woven in black and navy blue, this elegant *obi* was possibly part of a mourning dress ensemble and worn with a plain black kimono. Known as *mofuku*, funereal dress is distinguished from other black formal dress by having completely dark accessories with minimal adornment.

This lavish pre-tied *obi* (*tsuke-obi*) is arranged in the *fukura suzume* (plum-sparrow) knot. Made from vermilion-ground polychrome figured silk, it is patterned with floral roundels floating on rippling water. An *obi* pillow (*obi-makura*) nestles within the *obi* knot, which has hooks into the corresponding pre-folded sash. The white cords of the sash section are used to tie the sash and would be concealed when worn. This *tsuke-obi* set was part of a kimono ensemble given by a daughter of the emperor of Japan to a member of the British royal family in the early 1960s.

Obi for a woman
Polychrome figured silk
1960s

Given anonymously
FE.76:1, 2-2012

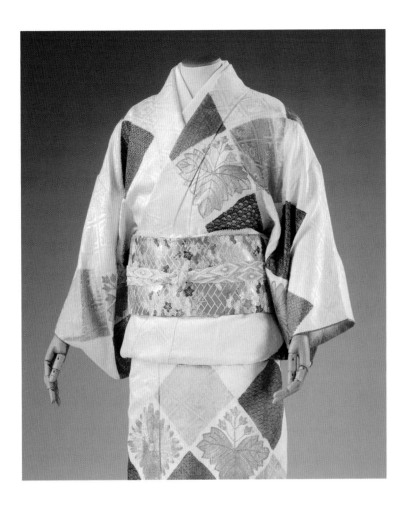

The sophisticated yet unexpected colour combinations found in Japanese dress can be seen in this *obi-jime* of lime green, gold and white, which would have been worn with the vermilion-ground polychrome-figured silk *tsuke-obi* on p. 123 or the gold-ground *obi* above. Finely braided silk cords such as this are known as *kumihimo* and are generally used to secure *obi*. This style of *kumihimo* – flat with diamond pattern – is called *kara gumi*. *Kumihimo* are braided on a round stand (*marudai*). Since Japanese dress has no fastenings, ties such as this are an integral part of an ensemble, resulting in a varied array of cords that are both decorative and functional.

Obi-cord for a woman (*obi-jime*)
Braided silk; metallic thread
1960s

Given anonymously
FE.80-2012

Obi belt for a man
Leather and metal (belt);
plain-weave printed cotton (kimono)
Belt: 2016; kimono: Tokyo, 2017

Robe Japonica

FE.40-2018, FE.38-2018

A thick hip-slung belt functions as an *obi* with this informal cotton kimono (*yukata*), both by Tokyo-based label Robe Japonica. The double row of studs on plain brown leather offer a military edge, complementing the repeat pattern of fighting samurai in red, mustard and brown, densely placed to resemble camouflage. Young designers such as Robe Japonica's Ueoka Tarō (b. 1965) are striving to make kimono more accessible for younger generations. Such bold designs for men's kimono are reflective of the burgeoning market for male Japanese dress. Incorporating simple features, such as a belt, enable people to wear kimono even if they are unable to tie an *obi*.

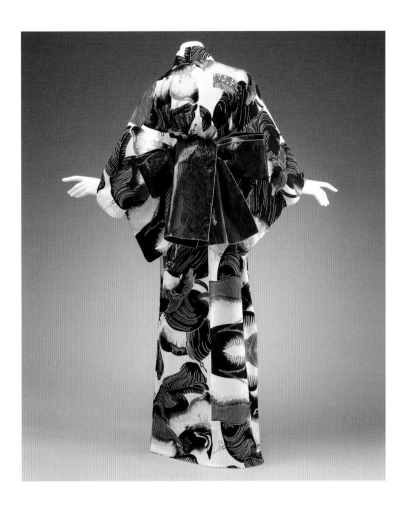

The most informal style of *obi* is the *heko obi,* a soft fabric sash that is usually worn with cotton summer kimono (*yukata*). While most *heko obi* are made from silk crêpe (*chirimen*), this glittering example by Rumi Rock is made from ribbed lamé. The double-sided colour way of red and black make it reversible, but also allows the wearer to arrange the *obi* to reveal both sides. At the upper edge, the brand's name is written in cursive Gothic script, while the lower edge is bordered with a scrolling floral pattern. Unlike more formal *obi* styles, the *heko obi* can be tied using just a simple knot or a more decorative bow. This *obi* is particularly striking when styled with this Rumi Rock stencil-dyed summer-wear kimono (*yukata*), patterned with Edo period hairstyles. Rumi Rock is proudly located in what was the Yoshiwara, the former licensed quarters of Tokyo. Founded by Shibasaki Rumi (b. 1965), the brand specializes in hand-crafted *yukata* that combine Edo sensibilities with rock-'n'-roll style.

Obi for a woman

Obi: polyester lamé; kimono: stencil-dyed plain-weave cotton
Tokyo, 2018
Rumi Rock
FE.3-2019, FE.2-2019

This playful waist sash is a style known as 'Nagoya *obi*'. Named after the city in which it supposedly developed, the Nagoya *obi* is now one of the most commonly worn types of sash. Three quarters of the *obi* are folded and sewn in place, making it easier to put on. It is usually tied using the *otaiko* (drum) knot secured with a further narrow sash (*obi-age*), tied above the *obi*, and a cord (*obi-jime*) tied in the middle. In this ensemble, the *obi-age* is silk crêpe embroidered with the brand name, Mamechiyo Modern, while the *obi-jime* is worn with a decorative accessory called an *obi-dome* in the form of a butterfly. The patterns on Nagoya *obi*, such as these anthropomorphic rabbits, are carefully placed in both horizontal and vertical orientations so that they are revealed in their entirety when tied. Mayanaga Kumiko is a contemporary kimono designer who specializes in nostalgic style and gives her pieces whimsical names such as this example, which is titled *Mademoiselle Ravi*.

Obi for a woman
Printed silk; polyester lining
2011
Mamechiyo Modern
FE.296-2011

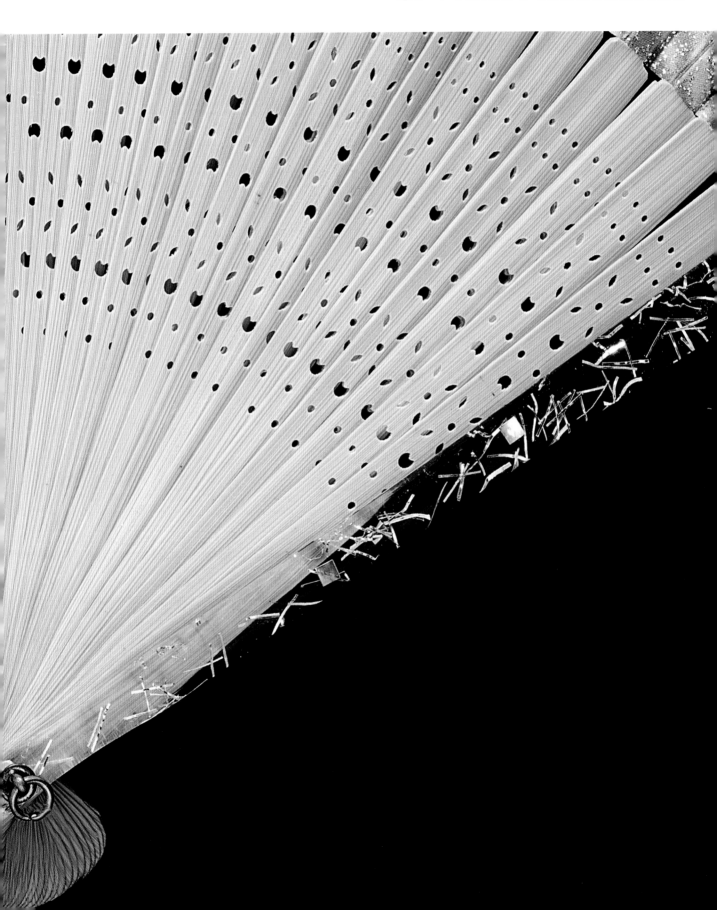

5. Waist Accessories

Fan print (*uchiwa-e*)
The Niwaka Festival in the Yoshiwara
Utagawa Kuniyoshi (1797–1861)
Colour print from woodblocks
1850–2

E.12123-1886

One style of fan popular in Japan is the *uchiwa*, a rigid hand fan that is usually made of paper stuck to a wooden support. This form led to a printmaking genre known as *uchiwa-e* (fan prints) and many famous artists made designs for fans. Like the images associated with contemporary life (*ukiyo-e*), landscapes, famous actors and beautiful women were popular subject matter for fan prints. An essential item in the hot and humid Japanese summer, *uchiwa* are associated with festivals, one of which, the Niwaka, is depicted here. Being held in the Yoshiwara, the licensed pleasure quarter of Edo (now Tokyo), this woman is probably a courtesan. Shown coquettishly holding a folding fan, this self-referential image cleverly advertises both the courtesan and this accessory.

Folding fan (*sensu*)
Carved and pierced bamboo;
paper; acrylic; metal
1950s

Given by Leslie Howard
FE.51-2017

Dating back to the Heian period, fans are attractive accessories and have been widely used for ceremonial, performance and practical purposes. They continue to be common features of Japanese dress. Made from carved and pierced bamboo sticks, this folding fan has touches of glitter on both the mounted paper and suspended within the acrylic outer sticks. The asymmetric design of a single purple iris is both elegant and suitable for a fan as the flower blooms in early summer. When not in use, folded fans are often tucked into the waist sash (*obi*). Japanese folding fans have had a significant influence on European fashion since their introduction via the Silk Road trade in the latter half of the 16th century.

Mount Atago, from the series
Famous Views of Edo Matched
with Hokku Poems
Utagawa Kunisada (1786–1864)
Colour print from woodblocks
Edo (Tokyo), 1843–7

Given by the Misses Alexander
E.6089-1916

Amulets for children
(Omamori bukuro)
Polychrome figured silk; embroidery
in silk and metallic threads; braided silk
1850–1900

Given by Count Mutsu Hirokichi
T.302-1910

Plain-weave stencil-dyed silk;
braided silk cord
1850–1900

Given by Charles Lund, Esq.
545-1908

These small decorative pouches are amulets for children (*Omamori bukuro*) to be worn from their *obi* when playing outside. Amulets such as this often contain a prayer written on paper, but these examples also contain rice grain as a religious offering. Both pouches have large silk braids secured in the form of an eternal knot. One is made from stencil-dyed plain-weave silk with stylized flowers, the other elaborately woven with coloured silk and metallic threads and partly embroidered with a carp and basket. Carp are popular symbols in Japan for not only do they swim against the current but, according to legend, are able to leap the waterfall at Dragon's Gate, thereby transforming themselves into divine creatures. Carp were considered suitable motifs for boys, conveying the courage and strength that parents hoped their sons would have for their future life. This *Omamori bukuro* was given to the museum by Count Mutsu Hirokichi (1869–1942), a Japanese diplomat and key figure in orchestrating the Japan-British Exhibition of 1910 in White City, London. It might have been worn by Mutsu's son Ian (1907–2002) before it was given to the Victoria and Albert Museum.

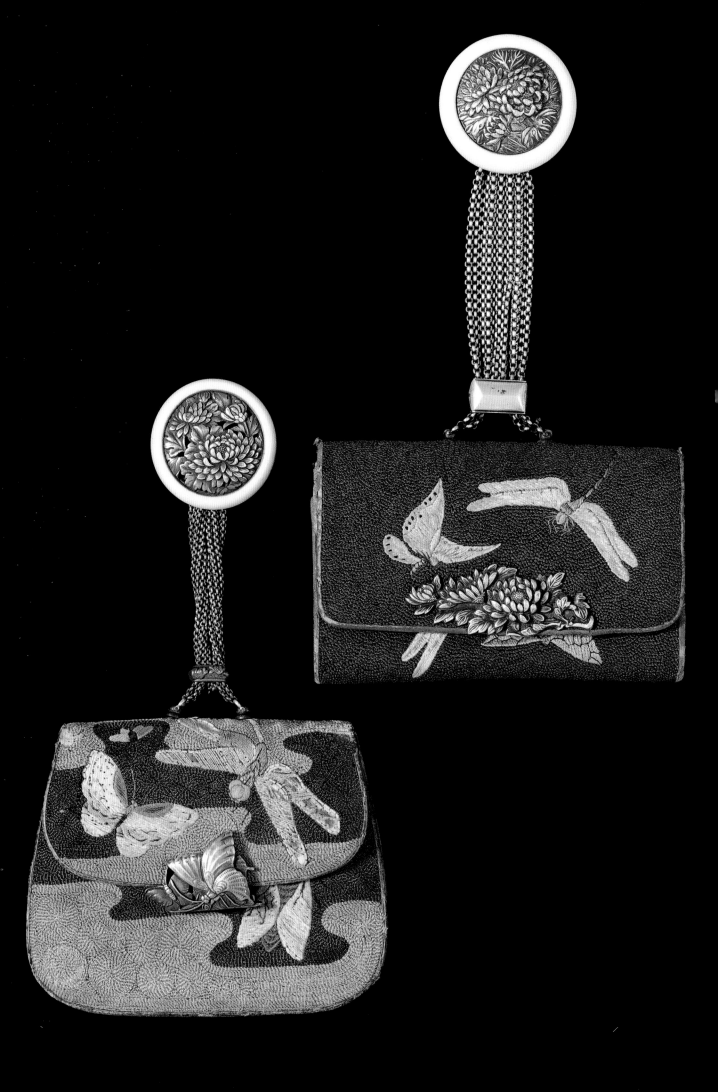

Butterflies and dragonflies, auspicious symbols representing longevity and courage respectively, adorn these densely embroidered tobacco pouches. The pouch pictured on the left has a background of clouds embroidered in couched circles of twisted blue and beige threads interspersed with various insects while the silvered-metal clasp (*mae-kanagu*) is formed of two silver butterflies. In the other pouch blue knot stiches (*sagara-nui*) form a solid ground and a bunch of silver chrysanthemums form the clasp. At the top of both pouches are silver suspension chains attached to the toggles (*netsuke*). These are in the *kagamibuta* (mirror-lid) style consisting of an ivory bowl and silvered metal 'mirror lids' decorated with chrysanthemums cast in high relief. These would have been worn suspended from an *obi* worn around the waist.

*Gathering Mushrooms
in Mid-Autumn*
Utagawa Kunisada (1786–1864)
Colour print from woodblocks
Edo (Tokyo), 1843–7

Given by the Misses Alexander
E.6076-1916

OPPOSITE

Tobacco pouches
Leather covered with linen;
embroidery in silk; silver; ivory
1850–1900

T.124-1964

Given by Miss J. Gudgeon
T.383-1977

**Dress accessory for a man
(*inrō*, *netsuke* and *ojime*)**
Wood with black, gold and silver
takamaki-e lacquer and mother-of-pearl
inlay (*raden*)

Signed Tokei, 1750–1850

Pfungst Gift
W.221:1,2, 3-1922

Traditional forms of Japanese dress such as the kimono did not have
pockets. A man would carry everyday items in containers such as
inrō that were worn suspended from the *obi*, secured with a *netsuke*
(toggle) and *ojime* (bead). While the original purpose of the *inrō*
was a container for ink seals or medicines, they became essentially
fashionable, rather than functional, accessories. This *inrō* is made
of lacquer on wood and decorated with two dance masks, a motif
repeated on the *netsuke* and *ojime*. It is unusual to find a coordinated
set of *inrō*, *netsuke* and *ojime* such as this.

**Dress accessories for men
(*inrō, netsuke* and *ojime*)**
Inrō: black lacquer with gold and
silver *togidashi maki-e* lacquer;
ojime: ivory
Signed Koma Kyūhaku, 1775–1850
Pfungst Gift
W.164:1,2-1922

Inrō: black, gold, silver and red
takamaki-e lacquer; *netsuke*: carved
staghorn; *ojime*: wood; ivory
Signed Koma Yasutada, 1750–1850
W.116:1,2,3-1922

Inrō: black lacquer; mother-of-pearl;
gold foil; *netsuke*: black lacquer;
mother-of-pearl; *ojime*: hardstone
Signed Yamada Jōka, 1775–1850
Pfungst Gift
W.238:1,2,3-1922

Inrō: black, gold and red *togidashi
maki-e* lacquer; *netsuke*: carved wood;
ojime: metal
Signed Toshihide (*inrō*) and Miwa
(*netsuke*), 1800–50
Pfungst Gift
W.236:1,2,3-1922

The vast array of *inrō* made during the Edo period reveal how popular
this item of male fashionable dress was. Most *inrō* were made from
lacquer, an expensive and time-consuming technique that produces a
lustrous surface, often further embellished with inlaid shell, hardstones
or precious metals. Of the various decorative techniques, the most
lavish is *maki-e*, in which the design is sprinkled onto wet lacquer.
The three main types of *maki-e* are *hiramaki-e* (low-sprinkled picture),
takamaki-e (high-sprinkled picture) and *togidashi maki-e* (polished-out
picture). *Inrō* were also made of shell, ivory, metal, ceramic and precious
stone. Subject matter also varied greatly, from designs reflecting daily
life in the style of woodblock prints (*ukiyo-e*) to folk tales and myths and
painterly depictions of the natural world. The intricate and elaborate
decoration on many *inrō* indicate that these were made to be admired
as markers of affluence, rather than functional items of dress. The
Victoria and Albert Museum has around 900 *inrō* in the collection, many
of which were gifts or bequests to the museum by British collectors,
such as this selection that were all given by Richard A. Pfungst in 1922.

Kimono for a girl
Plain-weave silk; freehand paste
resist-dyeing (*yūzen*)
Probably Kyoto, 1800–50

FE.191-2018

The literary subject matter and muted colours of this girl's kimono
reveal how similar children's dress was to that of adults during the
Edo period. Decorated in the *goshodoki* (palace-court) style,
this kimono would have been worn by a young girl of samurai rank.
The scene depicted is associated with *The Tales of Genji*, the most
famous Japanese work of classical literature written by Murasaki Shikibu
in the 11th century and widely acknowledged as the world's first novel.
At the hem, a dropped fan sits on a palatial veranda, the corner of
which juts out from a clouded autumnal landscape, the textile partition
(*kichō*) flowing in the wind. The undyed sections (*shiroage*), which
were drawn with rice paste, provide linear definition while pigments
have been applied in certain parts for added detail and variety.

Outer kimono for a woman (*uchikake*)
Plain-weave silk crêpe (*chirimen*); hand-painting; stencil-dyeing (*kata-yūzen*); embroidery in silk threads
Probably Kyoto, 1860–1900

Murray Bequest
T.389-1910

Rather than plain red silk, maple leaves floating on rippling water decorate the pale blue hem of this graceful outer kimono, adding to the painterly quality of the overall garment. Above this subtle detail, a pair of cranes surrounded by plum blossom stand in front of a pine tree. The entire surface of the garment has been treated as a canvas, which incorporates hand-painting and stencil-dyeing (*kata-zome*). Parts of the picture are highlighted with embroidery. Believed to live for 1,000 years, cranes are a symbol of longevity, which suggests that this may have been a bridal garment.

Outer kimono for a woman (*uchikake*)

Silk satin (*shusu*); appliqué; embroidery in silk and metallic threads

Probably Kyoto, 1850–1900

FE.73-2014

This exuberant outer kimono (*uchikake*) has a thick wadded hem, which is designed to trail on the ground and create an elongated silhouette. The padded area is covered in polychrome figured silk, however, many of the supplementary wefts have been lost through wear. The underside is lined with plain-weave red cotton that was probably added later to protect the hem from further damage. The rest of the kimono is made from black silk satin with appliqué and embroidery in silk and metal-wrapped threads depicting scenes from the well-known play *Shakkyō* (*The Stone Bridge*). *Shishi* (mythical lions) dance among the peonies below a bridge, symbols of the Pure Land at Mount Shōryōzen and destination of the story's protagonist, the monk Jakushō. This garment was probably worn by a high-ranking courtesan.

The damage caused by lining hems, particularly those designed to trail on the floor, with delicate silk is evident on this outer kimono (*uchikake*), which has been heavily restored and conserved. Plain-weave red silk (*habotae*) is most commonly used to line hems of *uchikake*, often providing an alluring contrast to the fabric used for the kimono. In this example, a rich blue satin ground is lavishly embroidered all over with ducks on rippling water amongst seasonal flowers. This kimono was probably worn by a bride on her wedding day. Ducks (*oshidori*) are a popular motif on Japanese bridal kimono as the birds are thought to mate for life. Happily married people are still likened to ducks through the Japanese phrase *oshidori fufu* (duck couple).

Outer kimono for a woman (*uchikake*)

Silk satin (*shusu*); embroidery in silk and metallic threads
Probably Kyoto, 1800–50

Given by Mr T.B. Clark-Thornhill
T.79-1927

Kimono for a woman
Plain-weave silk crêpe (*chirimen*);
tie-dyeing (*shibori*); freehand paste
resist-dyeing (*yūzen*); embroidery in silk
and metallic threads
Probably Kyoto, 1910–30

FE.19-2014

An elderly man enjoys food and sake while watching kimono-clad sparrows dance within a bamboo grove on the lower half of this striking black kimono. The beguiling scene is from the famous Japanese fairy tale, *Shita-kiri Suzume* (*The Tongue-cut Sparrow*). This tells the tale of a kind woodcutter who finds an injured sparrow. While nursing it back to health, his jealous wife cuts the tongue of the sparrow and sends it back into the wild. The woodcutter goes to look for his friend and finds the sparrow in a bamboo grove, where the bird has prepared a feast for the man. While he eats, other birds dance for him. As a gift, the sparrow offers the woodcutter one of two baskets. Not wishing to be greedy, the woodcutter choses the smaller one and when he arrives home is amazed to find it full of treasure. His wife, annoyed that he had not chosen the bigger basket, goes herself in search of the sparrow she had harmed. She is greeted kindly by the birds and given the large basket. Eager for the wealth she assumes it contains, the woman opens the basket on the way home only to discover it is full of monsters and ghosts. She is so surprised and scared that she tumbles to her death.

Kimono for a young woman (*furisode*)

Plain-weave silk crêpe (*chirimen*);
freehand paste resist-dyeing (*yūzen*);
embroidery in silk threads
Probably Kyoto, 1890–1910

Given by Lady Palairet in memory
of Sir Michael Palairet
T.266-1968

Pine tree boughs among golden clouds decorate the hem and sleeve ends of this sophisticated kimono. Created using the freehand resist-dye method (*yūzen*), such minimal but striking patterning contrasts with the vast expanse of black that covers the rest of the body. By the end of the 19th century, patterns were mostly concentrated at the hem of a kimono while the early 20th century witnessed a fashion for such deeply saturated colours that were more easily produced by aniline dyes. The five crests on the back and shoulders indicate that this is a highly formal garment while the long sleeves suggest it was for an unmarried woman, possibly worn at her wedding day. For a bride, a kimono such as this would have been the height of understated elegance.

Graceful blades of pampas grass frame the hem of this enchanting kimono which, among other autumnal motifs, has a small white rabbit leaping into the scene from the seam on the right. The skilful combining of two different dyed effects – delicate shading in the background and the main design in free-hand paste resist – creates depth, further heightened by the small areas of embroidery such as the rabbit, outlines of the leaves, and flowerheads. Even the figured ground – a repeat pattern of clouds – contributes to the overall pictorial quality. The highly patterned hem contrasts with the subtle shading of a full moon on the shoulder. In East Asian folklore the markings on the moon have been read as a rabbit with pestle and mortar, making the animal a popular symbol for the autumn equinox.

Kimono for a woman
Figured silk crêpe (*mon chirimen*); freehand paste resist-dyeing (*yūzen*); embroidery in silk and metallic threads
Probably Kyoto, 1912–26

FE.23-2014

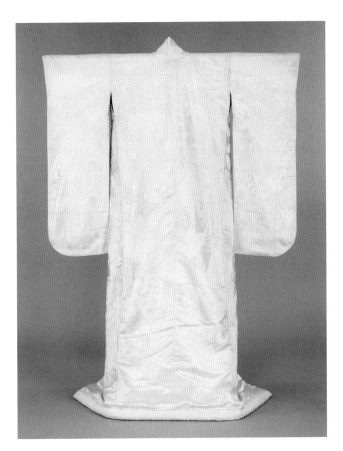
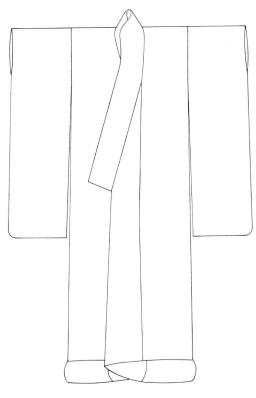

Luxurious layers of ivory silk make up this elaborate bridal ensemble. Below the heavily padded hem of the outer kimono (*uchikake*) is a double-layered bridal kimono (*kakeshita*) with a lightly padded hem, designed so that each section is visible when worn. The folds beautifully echo the woven pattern of a *tabane noshi*, an auspicious motif of bundled abalone strips. *Tabane noshi* were once offerings to the gods and are now made of paper and attached to gifts. On kimono, the form makes a striking motif as the ribbons billow out from the central knot over the shoulders and down the sleeves, each section woven with a different decorative pattern. In contrast, the kimono below has a repeat geometric key-fret pattern and plain underlayer. All-white bridal ensembles such as this are called *shiromuku* and are worn for the first part of a wedding ceremony.

Kimono ensemble for a bride (*shiromuku*)
Monochrome woven silk
1980–2000

Given by Moe Co. Ltd
FE.154-2002; FE.152-2002

This kimono has a very striking lining, a marker of secret luxury that would only have been glimpsed as the woman walked along. The delicate design of plum blossoms on the outside contrasts with the bold combination of lime green and bright red on the inside. The green silk is woven with a pattern that represents rippling water, the curving shapes echoed in the outline of the fabric on the red silk crêpe that is embroidered in gold with scattered flowers. The plum motif is a popular design for winter dress such as this outer kimono as the tree is the first to blossom in the New Year. The theme on the lining, of blossoms falling by a riverside, is also suggestive of the coming pleasures of springtime.

Outer kimono for a young woman (*uchikake*)
Polychrome figured silk; lining of monochrome figured twill silk (*mon aya*); silk crêpe (*chirimen*); embroidery in metallic threads
Probably Kyoto, 1860–80

Given by Mr T.B. Clark-Thornhill
T.78-1927

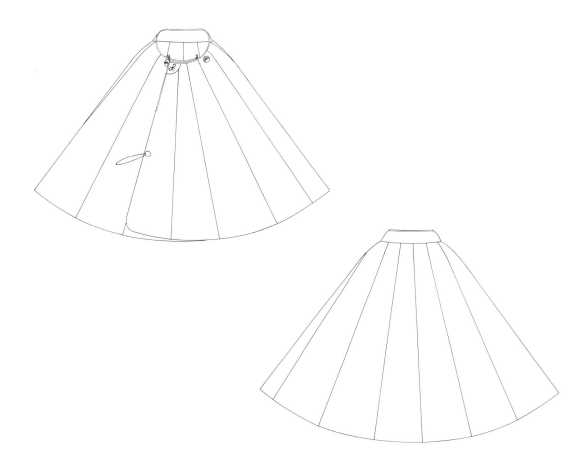

Travel cape for a man (*bōzukappa*)
Plain-weave cotton; resist-dyed
1850–1900

FE.1-1988

Indigo-dyed cotton fabrics are synonymous with everyday life in 19th-century Japan. The popular blue dye has been used on both the outer and inner fabrics of this cape. One side has been patterned with the *kasuri* technique, in which the yarns are selectively dyed prior to weaving. The other side is elegantly striped in blues, black and orange. The garment, known in Japan as a *bōzukappa*, is constructed from 16 triangular sections of cotton with a short upright collar fitted at the neck. The style was adapted from capes worn by Portuguese missionaries in Japan in the 16th century, the name deriving from *bōzu*, the Japanese for priest, and *kappa*, the Japanese transliteration of the Portuguese for cape.

Coordinated double-layered kimono sets such as this were fashionable in the mid-Meiji period. The softly shaded grey silk crêpe and subtle decoration of this example are also typical features of the time. Rather than reference classical literature, the small-scale pattern at the hem depicts a pastoral scene of tea pickers. The minutiae of daily life are beautifully rendered, including a young child and puppy, embellished with touches of bright pink embroidery, in the part of the ensemble that would only be visible when the wearer moved. In stark contrast to the pale grey ground is the red lining of the outer kimono and body of the under kimono (*dōnuki*), the latter with a clamp resist-dyed (*itajime*) pattern of cherry blossoms.

Layered kimono set for a woman (*kasane*)
Plain-weave silk crêpe (*chirimen*); freehand paste resist-dyeing (*yūzen*) and clamp resist-dyed lining (*itajime*); embroidery in silk threads
Probably Kyoto, 1880–1900

FE.18:1,2-2014

Under kimono for a woman (*dōnuki*)
Plain-weave silk crêpe (*chirimen*);
stencil printed (*kata-yūzen*)
and resist-dyed (*shibori*)
1890–1910

FE.21-2014

Various patterns in tones of blue and grey have been patched together to make this attractive under kimono. While four different fabrics have been used, only the black and white fabric, which has been used for the collar, sleeve edges and hem, would have been visible and possibly coordinated with a matching kimono made in the same fabric. This small-scale design of flying cranes is stencil printed, as is the pale blue spotted fabric on the sleeves. A section of indigo tie-dyed silk crêpe features around the waist while the upper body is plain green crêpe. This type of under kimono, which is made to match the kimono, is known as a *dōnuki*. While many were made using brightly coloured and contrasting fabrics, such as the one of the previous page, subtle patchwork examples were also popular.

Under kimono for a woman (naga-juban)
Figured silk satin (*rinzu*); stencil printed (*kata-yūzen*)
1920–50

FE.14-1987

Bamboo and plum blossom nestle among stylized clouds on this striking under kimono (*naga-juban*). The plain white collar, which was probably covered with a decorative half collar (*han-eri*), contrasts with the highly patterned fabric of the body. Glimpses of this would have been visible at the sleeve openings and hem when the wearer moved. Woven with a large-scale key-fret pattern, the fabric has been stencil printed with a bold pattern in blue, yellow, red and green on a black ground. Such vibrant designs are typical of early 20th-century kimono fashion, a style that extended to undergarments.

The dynamic design on this man's under kimono reflects the increasing nationalism of Japan during the 1930s. Patriotism was of great importance as the nation's imperial ambitions were aggressively pursued in Asia and such sentiments even affected dress. The novelty prints of more peaceful times (compare with that on p. 174) were transformed into propaganda motifs, such as in this garment that features battleships and warplanes with searchlights. Having such a design on an undergarment suggests that the wartime cause was close to the wearer's heart.

Under kimono for a man (*naga-juban*)
Plain-weave silk; stencil printed (*kata-yūzen*)
1930–40
FE.44-2014

Men's garments tend to be plain and sombre in comparison with those for women. However, there is an exception for *haori* linings, which can have lively designs such as this example. Within this black-crested *haori* is a printed silk lining with a Cubist-style arrangement of musical instruments including guitar, trombone and banjo. Such instruments suggest jazz, the musical genre that defined early 20th-century culture. Urban Japan was transformed in the early 20th century by the introduction of cafés, dance halls and cinemas, and as a result the Taishō period is often described as Japan's jazz age. Such lively linings can be seen as a modern interpretation of Edo-period fashions for concealed decoration that arose to subvert sumptuary laws.

Kimono jacket for a man (*haori*)
Plain-weave silk; stencil printed
(*kata-yūzen*)
1930s
FE.26-2016

Kimono jacket for a man (*haori*)
Plain-weave silk with silk woven with
selectively pre-dyed yarns (*kasuri*);
polychrome figured silk
1910–31

FE.28-2016

The most preeminent jazz-age motif, an LP record, is woven into the
lining of this *haori*. The grooves are delineated in contrasting colours
creating a sense of movement. Within the centre of the LP is a label
for Nipponophone records with their logo: an eagle with outstretched
wings. To the right of the record is a bottle of saké, the combination
of the two conveying a sense of relaxed sophistication. Nipponophone
was founded in 1910 and in 1931 affiliated with the Columbia Graphophone
Company of the United Kingdom, changing its name to Nippon
Columbia Co., Ltd in 1946.

Kimono jacket for a man (*haori*)
Plain-weave silk; stencil printed
(*kata-yūzen*)
1920–40
FE.29-2016

Aeroplanes and a zeppelin fly above the towering skyscrapers of this modern metropolis that could as easily be New York as it is Tokyo. After the Great Kantō earthquake of 1923, which devastated the Japanese capital, the city was rebuilt to reflect international architectural styles such as art deco. The design cleverly incorporates the searchlights flashing through the clouds, creating a vivid and evocative evening scene. At this point, most urban Japanese men wore western style clothing, however, many wore Japanese dress in their leisure time. Such a modern, urban lining suggests that the wearer of this *haori* retained a sense of cosmopolitanism when wearing a kimono.

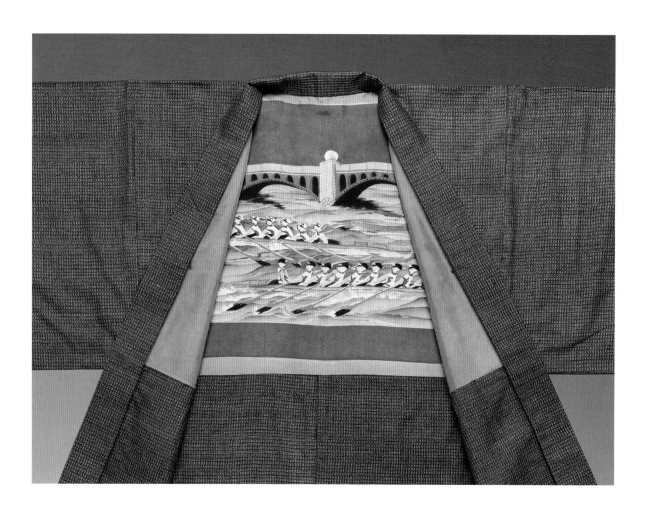

Kimono jacket for a man (*haori*)
Plain-weave silk with silk woven with
selectively pre-dyed yarns (*kasuri*);
stencil printed (*kata-yūzen*)
1930s

FE.27-2016

Not only does the woven silk outer fabric of this *haori* look like tweed,
the lining subject matter also suggests a British influence. At first
glance, the scene appears to be the famous Oxford and Cambridge
Boat Race; however, it is actually the Sokei Regatta on the Sumida
River in Tokyo. Inspired by the British example, the Sokei Regatta was
established in 1905 and involves two elite Tokyo universities, Waseda
and Keio. The dynamism of sporting activities made them popular Art
Deco motifs. This design seems to have been expressed through lively
brushstrokes but is, in fact, the result of stencil printing.

Stylized white camellias on a scarlet red ground decorate the lining on this otherwise simple garment. *Haori* were historically only worn by men, however, this changed in the 19th century when geisha adopted them and made the look fashionable. Although women's *haori* tend to be made in brightly patterned fabrics, thereby differentiating them from those for men, this plain black *haori* is distinguished as one for a woman by the lining. Camellias, a flower native to Japan, are popular motifs for Japanese dress and represent early spring.

Kimono jacket for a woman (*haori*)
Plain-weave silk; stencil printed
(*kata-yūzen*)
1950–70
Given by Miss D. Daniels
FE.142-1983

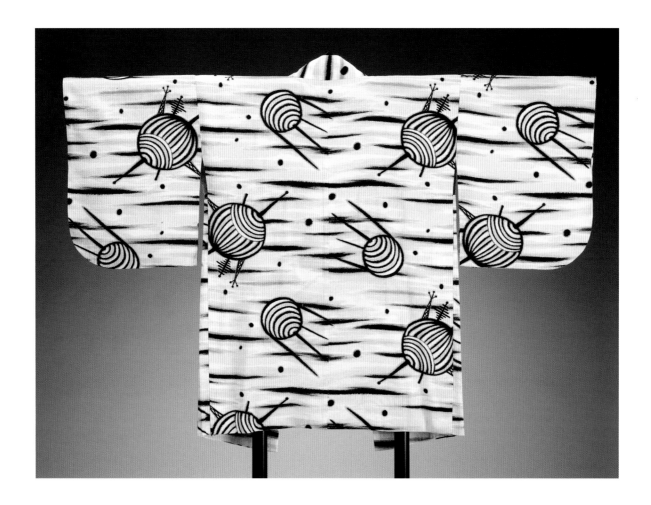

Kimono jacket for a woman (*haori*)
Plain-weave silk; stencil printed
(*kata-yūzen*)
c. 1957

FE.48-2014

Despite the overarching conservatism that pervaded kimono culture in the 1950s, some attempts were made to update kimono and make them relevant to current events. This example celebrates Sputnik I, an international phenomenon and the world's first artificial satellite, which was launched by the Soviet Union in October 1957. The bold stylized novelty print in pale pink and grey, vividly outlined in black, has a distinct influence of Populuxe – a portmanteaux of popular and luxury – a style fashionable in America in the 1950s and 1960s that blended futurism with optimism. This *haori* reveals the global reach of this space-age aesthetic. In contrast, the lining has the more traditionally feminine pattern of chrysanthemums on a pink ground.

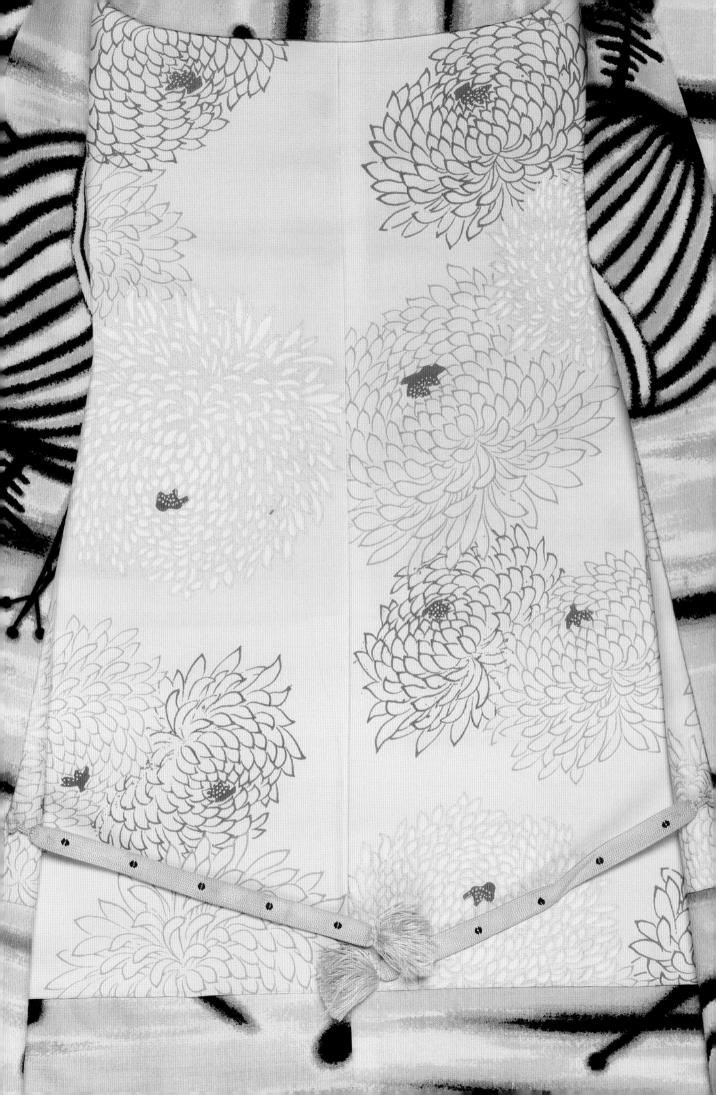

Pair of *geta* for a woman
Carved and lacquered wood; straw;
silk velvet; rabbit fur; metal
Probably Kyoto, 1920s

FE.11:1, 2-2015

Although mostly open and held to the foot by straps,
wooden footwear known as *geta* were worn throughout
the year in Japan. For affluent members of society,
the basic austerity of their style was tempered by
the addition of expensive materials. These luxurious
covered-toe *geta*, a type known as *yuki* (snow) *geta*,
combine comfort with style. The high red-lacquered
wooden supports, called *ha*, would have elevated the
wearer from the snow-covered ground, thus protecting
the hem of her kimono. Lacquer is impermeable to
liquid, making it an ideal coating for wet weather.
The soles are lined with woven straw and the thongs
are of red velvet, while the toe covers are made from
leather and lined with rabbit fur. Gold decoration at the
sides depicts cranes and pines, both auspicious motifs,
suggesting that these *geta* would have been worn at
a festive occasion, such as New Year celebrations.

Pair of *geta* for a woman
Carved and lacquered wood; silk woven
with selectively pre-dyed yarns (*kasuri*)
1930–40

FE.1:1, 2-2015

Covered in purple- and ivory-patterned velvet, these *geta* are a
fashionable take on a practical style. The uppers are made from ribbed
silk woven with selectively pre-dyed yarns (*kasuri*). The carved wooden
soles and teeth (*ha*) are coated in black lacquer painted with silver
maple leaves and stylized suggestions of water running along the
sides. They date from a period when fashionable dress became more
accessible to a broader section of society, with many styles drawing
on global aesthetics such as art deco. This pair was probably worn with
an informal yet stylish kimono.

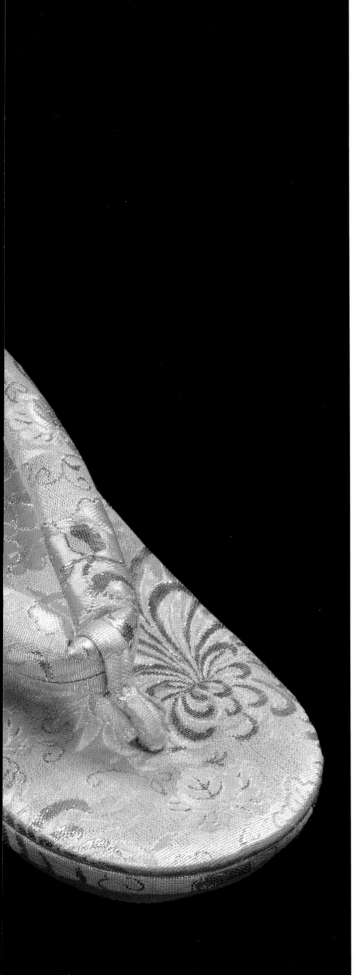

Pair of *zōri* for a woman
Twill weave with supplementary wefts; plastic
1950s
Given by Sarah Brooks in memory of her mother
Bernice Eileen (Wiese) Boo
FE.41:1, 2-2015

Zōri are fabric-covered sandals that are more formal
than *geta* and worn with *tabi* (split-toed socks). This
pair is made from figured silk woven with cream and
silver-gilt thread, with undersoles of plastic. The
elegant pattern of scrolling peonies, chrysanthemums
and paulownia leaves make them suitable for a variety
of kimono styles; however, the low height of the
stacked heal indicates that they are most appropriate
for semi-formal occasions. There are signs of wear
at the front base of the thongs that expose the twine
support below the fabric. This pair of *zōri* is part of a
kimono ensemble that belonged to Bernice Eileen Boo
(1930–2010; see p. 118).

**Compendium of Six Types of Flower
Likened to Young Women**
Utagawa Kunisada (1786–1864)
Colour print from woodblocks
Edo (Tokyo), 1843–7

Given by the Misses Alexander
E.6053-1916

Pair of *tabi* for a woman
Twill and plain-weave cotton; metal
1960s

Retailed by Mitsukoshi

Given anonymously
FE.84:1, 2-2012

Japanese dress is generally worn with split-toe socks called *tabi*. Specially designed to be worn with sandals, *tabi* are usually made from twill-weave cotton and cut to form for a snug fit. They have an opening at the back and are fastened at the ankle with a row of metal hook and eye closures known as *kohaze*. On this pair, the *kohaze* are embossed with the number 23.5 – the sole length measurement in centimetres – and the Mitsukoshi Department store logo, indicating from where they were purchased. The separated toe allows space for sandal thongs and the thick cotton provides protection for the otherwise exposed foot. As it is customary to remove footwear before entering homes and certain buildings, *tabi* have a reinforced sole to provide extra support. Although they are now available in a wide range of materials, plain white cotton is the most common fabric and the only style appropriate for formal occasions.

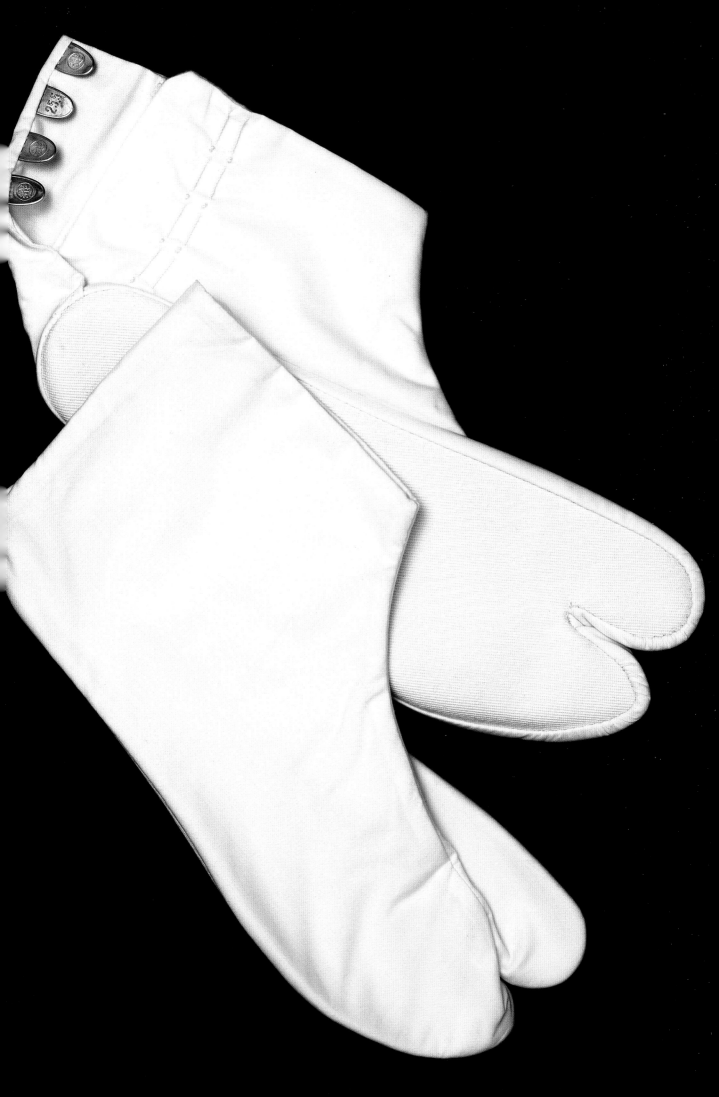

Pair of *waraji* for a man
Rice straw
1970s
Given by Rev. Zenkō Croysdale
FE.99:1, 2-2012

Waraji are made from rice straw rope and were once standard footwear for commoners and soldiers but are now chiefly worn by Buddhist monks, as was the case with this pair. The most utilitarian form of footwear, *waraji* consist of a thin woven sole with two long straps attached at the front, which are threaded through loops at the sides and heel, wrapped around the ankle and tied. When they were an essential part of a traveller's dress, *waraji* were often given to temples as part of prayers for safe journeys. Although they look uncomfortable, it is thought that they have significant health benefits, allowing for deft movement and strengthening of the legs.

Men's dress, including footwear, tends to be much plainer than that for women, but this pair of *geta* is exceptionally austere. Each *geta* is carved from a single block of wood and has thongs made of synthetic cream leather. They are an example of dress appropriate for a Zen monk and, together with the *waraji* opposite, were donated to the Museum by Zenkō Croysdale (1919–2007). Born in England as Charles G. Croysdale, Zenkō Croysdale lived as a Zen novice and priest in Japan from 1971–6, during which time he wore these shoes.

Pair of *geta* for a man
Carved wood; synthetic leather
1970s

Given by Rev. Zenkō Croysdale
FE.97:1, 2-2012

Pair of *geta* for a woman
Carved wood; embossed leather;
silk velvet; metal
Raven
Tokyo, 2009
Noritaka Tatehana

Given by Noritaka Tatehana
FE.51:1, 2-2012

Created by Noritaka Tatehana (b. 1985), this lavish
pair of *geta* create a circle when placed together.
A menacing black crow dominates the design, outlined
in gold on an emerald-green leather ground with
embossed *shippō* (seven-treasures) pattern and
red-velvet thongs. Ravens and crows (both translated
as *karasu*) hold a special place in Japanese mythology.
The three-legged crow (*yata-garasu*) is a messenger
of the Sun Goddess Amaterasu and is thought to have
guided Emperor Jinmu, the first emperor of Japan,
to victory in Yamato (present-day Nara). However, they
can also symbolize death and bad fortune. It was this
ominous association that inspired Tatehana, whose
graduate collection at the Tokyo School of Fine Art
was inspired by *oiran*, the high-ranking courtesans of
the Edo period who were considered the fashion icons
of their day. *Oiran* wore vertiginously high shoes as a
mark of their status, but also to protect the hems of
their lavish kimono.

The recent kimono revival has introduced fashionable updates to all aspects of Japanese dress, including *tabi* socks. This pair, made from black polyester lace, is more comfortable and practical than standard white cotton *tabi* as the stretch fabric negates the need for fastenings at the ankle. The openwork fabric makes them especially suited to wear during warmer months. While not appropriate for formal wear, they provide a playful and romantic touch to casual kimono. This pair was acquired to complete the Mamechiyo Modern ensemble featured above (also see pp. 130–1).

Pair of *tabi* for a woman
Polyester lace
2011
FE.301:1, 2-2011

Kimono ensemble
Crêpe polyester (kimono);
printed silk and polyester (*obi*); silk
crêpe (*obi-age*); braided silk (*obi-jime*);
resin (*obi-dome*); cotton velvet
(headress and necklace); vinyl,
velvet and lace (pair of shoes [*zori*]);
cotton and lace (bag)
2011
Mamechiyo Modern
FE.289 to FE.302-2011

Pair of *geta* for a girl
Carved and painted wood; straw;
silk velvet
Kyoto, 2000–10
FE.10:1, 2-2015

This pair of ceremonial *geta* has the onomatopoeic
name of *pokkuri*, a style mostly worn by young girls
and trainee geisha (*maiko*). They are defined by the
tall block base with slanted front, the heel of which
has been carved out. Within this cavity are bells that
chime when the wearer walks. The insoles are covered
in straw with red velvet thongs and the sides are
painted with a sedge of golden cranes in flight. This
pair is probably for a seven-year-old girl to wear to
her *shichi-go-san* (7-5-3) ceremony. The annual festival
takes place at Shinto shrines on 15 November and
celebrates the growth and well-being of young
children at these auspicious ages. For many children
today, *shichi-go-san* is their first experience of wearing
Japanese dress.

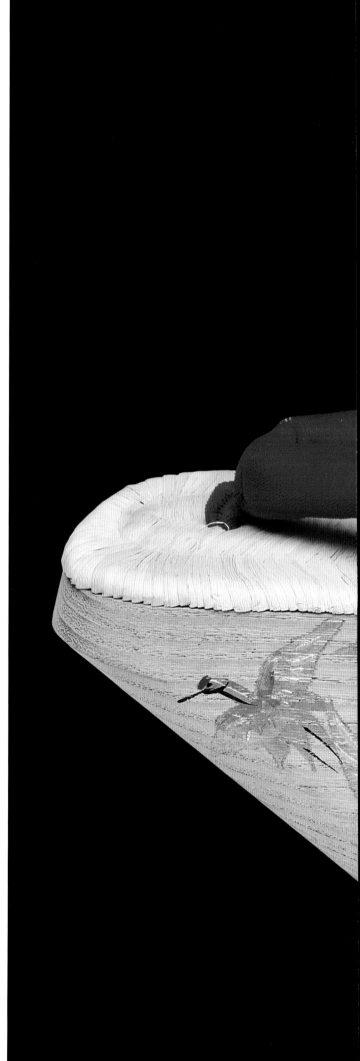

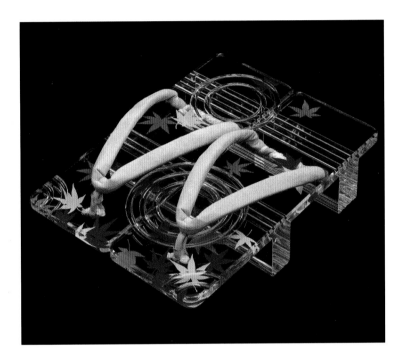

These contemporary men's sandals (*geta*) are made from transparent acrylic rather than wood, the material more commonly used for this style of footwear. The moulded design of concentric circles and lines cleverly creates the impression of raindrops on rippling water, overlaid with red, orange and yellow maple leaves. While they may seem strikingly modern, the motif has poetic origins. The image of fallen autumn leaves floating on the Tatsuta river features in the *Kokin Wakashū*, the earliest imperial anthology of Japanese poems (*waka*) first compiled around 905:

> A covering of
> Bright scattered leaves floats on the
> Tatsuta river –
> Were I to ford the waters
> The brocade would tear in half

Bearing an autumnal motif does not necessarily mean that these *geta* can only be worn during that season. Rather, they may be deemed more appropriate during the heat of summer to remind the wearer of the cooler months to come.

Pair of *geta* for a man
Moulded acrylic; leather
Tokyo, 2017
Robe Japonica
FE.42:1,2-2018

Pair of *zōri* for a woman
Vinyl; synthetic velvet; *faux* fur
Tokyo, 2016

Iroca

FE.37:1, 2-2018

Daring and unconventional, this pair of two-tone
vinyl sandals (*zōri*) challenges the notion that
Japanese dress is conservative. The five-layered
stacked sole is covered in contrasting metallic purple
and turquoise vinyl, on which the lime-green thongs
are almost completely obscured by white *faux* fur.
They are designed by Ishikawa Narutoshi (b. 1965)
for his contemporary kimono label Iroca. Ishikawa's
work is influenced by cyberpunk, a style affiliated with
dystopian futures and an unlikely influence for dress
associated with tradition and formality, such as *zōri*.
However, such a dynamic approach to Japanese dress
ensures it remains relevant for contemporary wearers.

Atkins, Jacqueline M., *Wearing Propaganda: Textiles on the Home Front in Japan, Britain and the United States 1931–1945* (New Haven, CT, and London 2006)

Blakemore, Frances, *Japanese Design Through Textile Patterns* (New York, NY, and Tokyo 1978)

Brandon, Reiko M., *Country Textiles of Japan: The Art of Tsutsugaki* (New York, NY, and Tokyo 1986)

— *Bright and Daring: Japanese Kimono in the Taishō Mode* (Honolulu 1996)

Cliffe, Sheila, *The Social Life of Kimono: Japanese Fashion Past and Present* (London 2017)

Dalby, Liza, *Kimono: Fashioning Culture* (New Haven, CT, and London 1993)

Faulkner, Rupert, *Japanese Studio Crafts: Tradition and the Avant-Garde* (London 1995)

Gluckman, Dale Carolyn and Sharon Sadako Takeda, *When Art Became Fashion: Kosode in Edo-Period Japan* (Los Angeles, CA, 1992)

Hauge, Victor and Takako, *Folk Traditions in Japanese Art* (Tokyo, New York, NY, and San Francisco, CA, 1978)

Howell Smith, A.D., *Guide to the Japanese Textiles. Part I: Textile Fabrics* (London 1919)

Hutt, Julia and Hélène Alexander, *Ogi: The History of the Japanese Fan* (London 1919)

Ikegami, Eiko, *Bonds of Civility: Aesthetic Networks and the Political Origins of Japanese Culture* (Cambridge 2005)

Jackson, Anna, *Japanese Country Textiles* (London and New York, NY, 1997)

— *Japanese Textiles in the Victoria and Albert Museum* (London 2000)

— Japanese costume entries in Crill, Rosemary, Jennifer Wearden and Verity Wilson (eds), *Dress in Detail from around the World* (London 2002)

— 'Ritual and Drama: Japanese Costume in the Victoria and Albert Museum', *Arts of Asia*, vol. 33, no. 2, 2003, pp. 102–9

— 'Dynamic lines and Syncopated Rhythms: Art Nouveau and Art Deco Designs in Early Twentieth-Century Kimono', in Assche, Annie van (ed.), *Fashioning Kimono: Dress and Modernity in Early Twentieth-century Japan* (Milan 2005), pp. 30–7

— 'Fashion for the Foreign: The Taste for Exotic Textiles and Dress in Momoyama and Edo Period Japan', *Oriental Art*, vol. LV, no. 1, 2005, pp.28–36

Jackson, Anna (ed.), *Kimono: The Art and Evolutions of Japanese Dress – The Khalili Collection* (London 2015)

— *Kimono: Kyoto to Catwalk* (London 2020)

Japan Textile Colour Design Centre, *Textile Designs of Japan*. 3 vols (Tokyo and London 1980)

Kawakami, Shigeki and Yoko Woodson, *Four Centuries of Fashion: Classical Kimono from Kyoto National Museum* (San Francisco, CA, 1997)

Kennedy, Alan, *Japanese Costume: History and Tradition* (Paris 1990)

Koop, Albert J., *Guide to the Japanese Textiles. Part II: Costume* (London 1920)

Liddell, Jill, *The Story of the Kimono* (New York, NY, 1989)

Minnich, Helen Benton, *Japanese Costume and the Makers of its Elegant Tradition* (Rutland, VT, and Tokyo 1963)

Moes, Robert, *Mingei: Japanese Folk Art from the Montgomery Collection* (Alexandria, VA, 1995)

Munsterberg, Hugo, *The Japanese Kimono* (Oxford and Hong Kong 1996)

Nakano, Eisha and Barbara Stephan, *Japanese Stencil Dyeing: Paste Resist Techniques* (New York, NY, 1982)

Noma, Seiroku, *Japanese Costume and Textile Art* (The Heibonsha Survey of Japanese Art, vol. 16), (New York, NY, and Tokyo 1974)

Rathbun, William Jay, *Beyond the Tanabata Bridge: Traditional Japanese Textiles* (New York, NY, 1993)

Satsuki Milhaupt, Terry, *Kimono: A Modern History* (London 2014)

Stinchecum, Amanda M., *Kosode: 16th–19th Century Textiles from the Nomura Collection* (New York, NY, 1984)

Tomita, Jun and Noriko Tomita, *Japanese Ikat Weaving: The Technique of Kasuri* (London 1982)

Van Assche, Annie, *Fashioning Kimono: Art Deco and Modernism in Japan* (Milan 2005)

Wada, Yoshiko Iwamoto et al., *Shibori: The Inventive Art of Japanese Shaped Resist Dyeing* (Tokyo 1983)

Watson, William (ed.), *The Great Japan Exhibition, Art of the Edo Period 1600–1868* (London 1981)

Wilson, Verity, 'Country Textiles from Japan and the Ryukyu Islands (in the Victoria and Albert Museum)', *Orientations*, vol. 14, no. 7, July 1983, pp. 28–42

— 'Japanese Silk Textiles', *Orientations*, vol. 17, no. 12, December 1986, pp. 38–46

Yamanaka, Norio, *The Book of Kimono: The Complete Guide to Style and Wear* (Tokyo, New York, NY, and San Francisco, CA, 1982)

Yoshida, Shin-Ichiro and Dai Williams, *Riches from Rags: Saki Ori and Other Recycling Traditions in Japanese Rural Clothing* (San Francisco, CA, 1994)

Glossary

Atsuita Robe for the *Nō* theatre worn by actors playing male roles.

Bast fibres Made from the stem of plants such as hemp.

Bingata Stencil-dyed cotton made with mineral pigments for members of the Ryūkyūan royal family.

Bōzukappa Travelling cape.

Chirimen (crêpe) Weave structure in which untwisted warps are combined with tightly twisted wefts in plain weave resulting in a matt, textured fabric.

Dōnuki Under garment made of two or more fabrics. It is made to match the kimono.

Furisode 'Swinging-sleeve' kimono worn by young, unmarried women.

Geta Carved wooden sandals with thongs.

Han-eri Half collar to wear under kimono.

Hakama Divided lower garment described as either full-cut trousers or a divided skirt.

Haori Kimono-style jacket.

Hinagata-bon Sample books of kimono (*kosode*) designs published in the Edo period. The full term used to describe these books is '*kosode moyō hinagata-bon*'. The word *hinagata* refers to a miniaturized object or something created to serve as a model. *Moyō* means 'pattern' and bon means 'book'.

Hiramaki-e Basic form of *maki-e*, in which metal dust is sprinkled onto still-wet lacquer and then covered with a further layer of lacquer.

Hitoe Unlined silk kimono worn in summer.

Hōmongi Literally 'visiting wear', semi-formal kimono.

Inrō 'Seal basket', small decorative container worn hanging from the belt, often lacquered.

Itajime Resist-dyeing technique by which the fabric is clamped between wooden boards that are carved with a pattern.

Juban Under kimono.

Kabuki The popular drama of the Edo period.

Kamishimo Two-piece outfit worn by samurai consisting of *hakama* (pleated, divided lower garment described as either full-cut trousers or a divided skirt) and *kataginu* (sleeveless jacket with projecting shoulders).

Kanmuri Ceremonial headdress.

Kanzashi Hair ornaments.

Kariginu Hunting tunic worn at the imperial court and in *Nō* theatre.

Karaori Robe for the *Nō* theatre worn by actors playing female roles.

Kasane Layered kimono.

Kasuri Resist-dyeing technique in which warp and/or weft threads are pre-dyed so as to form patterns when the cloth is woven.

Katabira Summer kimono usually made of bast fibre.

Kata-yūzen Technique in which chemical dyes are mixed with rice paste and applied through stencils.

Katazome Technique in which rice paste is applied to woven fabric through stencils. Dyes do not penetrate the pasted areas.

Kazari-nui Auspicious stitches, often used on children's clothing.

Kimono The 'thing worn', the traditional Japanese garment for men and women.

Kinran Fabric woven with supplementary wefts of gold-covered thread.

Kirikane 'Cut metal', small squares of gold and silver used in lacquer decoration.

Kogin Hand-stitching technique of Tsugaru.

Kosode 'Small sleeve', the precursor of the kimono.

Maki-e 'Sprinkled picture', a technique of lacquer decoration. See also *hiramaki-e, takamaki-e* and *togidashi maki-e*.

Meisen Taffeta-like silk fabric that was very popular in the first half of the 20th century.

Michiyuki Literally 'while on the road', coat for a woman to be worn over kimono.

Mon Family crest or badge, often used as a decorative motif.

Netsuke Decorative toggle worn with *inrō*.

Nō Aristocratic drama originating in the 14th century.

Nui Japanese term for embroidery. Stitches include flat floss stitch (*hira-nui*), long and short stitches (*sashi-nui*) and knot stitch (*sagara-nui*). Embroidery with twisted threads is called *katayori*.

Obi Sash worn around the waist to secure the kimono.

Obi-age Sash worn around the waist above the *obi*.

Obi-jime Cord worn around the waist at the middle of the *obi*.

Obi-makura Pillow to support the *obi*.

Ojime Decorative bead used to secure and tighten the cords between the *netsuke* and *inrō*.

Omiyamairi Shintō rite of passage for infant children.

Omamori bukuro Amulet for children.

Openwork Work that is perforated or pierced.

Osōde Literally 'large sleeve', general term used to describe formal robes, with wide sleeve openings.

Plain weave Weave construction in which one warp thread passes over and under a single-weft thread.

Ra Type of gauze weave silk.

Raden Shell inlay.

Resist-dyeing Patterning of fabric or yarn by protecting selected areas from dye.

Rinzu Soft monochrome figured silk in which the ground and pattern are created by the juxtaposition of warp-faced and weft-faced satin weave areas.

Ro Type of silk gauze in which rows of plain weave alternate with one where adjacent warps are crossed.

Sashiko Form of quilting in which layers of cotton are sewn together with running stitch.

Sensu Folding fan.

Shibori Technique often equated with tie-dyeing in which sections of fabric are bound (*kanoko shibori*), stitched (*nuishime shibori*), sheathed, folded or clamped to protect them from penetration when the fabric is dyed.

Shibuici Copper-silver alloy.

Shintō The indigenous belief system of Japan, originally based on the veneration of natural phenomena.

Shōgun Military ruler of Japan from 1185 to 1868, in theory exercising his power with the consent of the emperor.

Sokutai Formal court dress.

Suri-hitta Stencil imitation *shibori* (also known as *kata kanoko*).

Tabi Split-toed socks.

Takamaki-e Form of *maki-e* in which lacquer is built up in relief with powdered clay or charcoal.

Takuhatsu-gasa Monk's hat for alms collecting.

Tie-dyeing Resist-dyeing technique in which certain parts of the fabric are tightly tied to prevent penetration by the dye.

Togidashi maki-e 'Polished-out picture', a form of lacquer decoration in which a *maki-e* design is covered over with several layers of lacquer of the same colour as the background. These layers are then polished down until the original design reappears, flush with the new background.

Uchikake Kimono with wadded hem worn without an *obi* over another kimono on formal occasions, usually in winter.

Uchiwa Non-folding hand fan.

Yukata Cotton kimono, worn for the bath or as informal summer wear.

Yūzen Resist-dyeing technique which involves drawing on cloth with paste extruded from a cloth bag that forms a protective barrier when dyes are brushed on. Named after the artist Miyazaki Yūzen (1654?–1736) who is credited with its invention.

Zori Fabric-covered sandals with thongs.

Acknowledgments

I would like to thank my colleagues at the Victoria and Albert Museum for their incredible help and support. I am especially grateful to Anna Jackson, Keeper of the Asian department for sharing her specialist knowledge with such generosity and her constant encouragement. It is on her research and writing that this book is based. My colleagues in the Asian department have all helped in numerous ways for which I am grateful.

Many thanks to Robert Auton for the stunning new photography and to Richard Davis for managing to schedule this into the Photo Studio's tight programme. I am also grateful to our wonderful Textiles Conservation, in particular Joanne Hackett, Elizabeth-Anne Haldane, Rachael Lee and Gesa Warner, who have all devoted not only their time and skills to this project but have injected it with passion and enthusiasm. Thanks as always to Richard Ashbridge and the Technical Services team.

Hannah Newell bravely took on this project, initiated by Kathryn Johnson, and I thank her greatly for her dedication, support and patience. Many thanks are due to Caroline Brooke Johnson for her excellent work as copy-editor, to Karolina Prymaka for her book design and Emma Woodiwiss for her sharp eye. Thank you to Susanna Ingram and Corinna Parker at Thames & Hudson for their expertise and support. I would also like to thank Caitlin Davies, the V&A Royal Literary Fund Writing Fellow for her advice and assistance.

Lastly, I would like to thank my family and friends.

Note

Names in the text are expressed in Japanese order: family name followed by given name. The exceptions are those with brand names and those who have an international profile whose names are more frequently written in western order.

Index